Visual Basic Programming for Kids

By Timothy Busbice

A book designed for 8-12 year olds to learn how to program a computer using Visual Studio.Net 2010

Visual Basic Programming for Kids

Written by Timothy Busbice

© 2010 by Timothy Busbice

All Rights reserved. No part of this work may be reproduced or transmitted in any form or by any means, electronic or mechanical, including photocopy, recording, or by information storage or retrieval system, without the prior written permission of the author.

Printed in the USA

May 2010 – First Edition

ISBN: 978-0-557-48703-5

Windows, Visual Basic, Visual Studio, Visual Studio.Net are trademarks of Microsoft Corp.

"Visual Basic Programming for Kids" is an independent publication and is not affiliated with, nor has it been authorized, sponsored, or otherwise approved by Microsoft Corporation.

The information contained in this book is distributed on an "as is" basis, without warranty. Although every precaution has been taken in the preparation of this work, the author assumes no responsibility for errors or omissions, or damages from the use of the information contained within.

This book is dedicated to my family from whom I find great strength

Table of Contents

Foreward 1
1. Let's Get Started 3
    Chapter 1 Definition Review 23
2. The Code Behind 25
    Chapter 2 Definition Review 44
3. Hangman 46
    The Code Behind 61
    Chapter 3 Definition Review 79
4. Tic Tac Toe 80
    Step 1: Learn It 81
    Step 2: Design It 82
    Step 3: Code It 84
        The Code Behind 96
    Step 4: Test and Tune It 119
    Step 5: Document It 125
    Step 6: Implement It 131
    Chapter 4 Definition Review 134
5. The Beginning 135
Index 136

Foreward

Good Parent, Guardian or Mentor Reading

I wrote this book when my 10 year old daughter came to me in January of 2010 and surprisingly told me that one of her goals this year was to learn how to program a computer. Being a Computer Scientist, I was very happy to hear my child wanting to learn some of the things I knew, and I immediately started to look for something that would help her begin the process of computer programming.

After an initial search, I could not find anything that seemed appropriate, and probably more importantly, would keep the interest of a 10 year old. There are some books available but all seemed to be very dry reading to me and I know my child well enough to know that the books I did review would cause her to lose her attention to other things very quickly. Therefore, I figured I would write my own book in a fashion that would hold a 10 year olds attention and allow them to learn the basics of programming.

Writing a book is one thing but determining the software language to write about is another. The first book I wrote was C# programming but I realize that not everyone wants to program in C#, and there are a lot of Visual Basic fans out there that would prefer their child learn what they know. So a likely book of course is Visual Basic programming.

It is very important, no matter what other programming techniques you may want your child to understand, that they have a good foundation. Visual Basic will give them just that. It is highly recommended that they use this book to learn Visual Basic first before learning ASP.NET (web development) or other languages.

This book has been tested using my daughter and her friends. They gave me great feedback which allowed me to change words and wording so they could understand. This book is kid tested!

What is important to me as the author is that kids can learn what a computer is about and how to program a computer at their level. I purposely left out a lot of information that most programming books would put in because I know this age group can and will lose interest very quickly. This book and the methods I use are to get a child programming immediately through example and try to explain concepts along the way. Someone ten years old, give or take, wants to jump into programming immediately and having to wade through several chapters of what programming concepts are, will lose the audience this book was designed for. So I apologize if you feel this book should give a better foundation of terms and definitions but there are plenty of books in the public domain that can give that to anyone who is interested.

Furthermore, this book is comprised of three simple programs that build upon the concepts of each. It starts out with a very simple program, moves to a little more complex and then into a slightly more complex program, each time giving a few more ideas and adding to the overall language nomenclature. This is truly an introduction by example but does lay a foundation to further study.

This book is full of Microsoft trademarks and I want to give Microsoft full credit for all it has done. This book assumes the reader has access to Microsoft Visual Studio 2010 or some other version of Visual Studio. If you do not have Visual Studio, please visit the Microsoft website (http://www.microsoft.com) and specifically http://www.microsoft.com/visualstudio to download and/or purchase a version of Visual Studio.Net.

In addition for assistance, code and more fun things to do, go to:

http://www.compscikids.com

1. Let's Get Started

If you were a computer, you would lie in bed until your Mom or Dad told you to wake up. But once you open your eyes, they would have to tell you to sit up, move your feet to the ground, stand up, move your right foot, move your left foot, right foot, left foot... This is what we have to do to make computers work. We have to wake them up and then tell them exactly what to do, step by step.

So computers are pretty dumb. They need us to create **programs** to tell them what to do and how to do it. Programs are simply a set of instructions or **statements**. Each statement performs a task and we put the statements in the order that we want them to run. So computers cannot do anything until we tell them what we want them to do, and in the sequence we lay it out for them, step by step. Just like I would not want to tell you to move your right foot forward if you were still lying in bed, when you write a program, you want to tell the computer what to do in the proper sequence. I would tell you to wake-up, sit up, put your feet on the floor, stand up and then move your right foot forward.

In the same way we must tell the computer what to do and in what order to do it, we must use a **language** that we and the computer can understand. If you're Mom or Dad spoke a language you did not know, they could tell you to do things and you would not understand what they were saying so you would end up lying in bed all day.

There are many computer languages. They have names like C, C#, C++, Pascal, Java, and many, many more. In this book, we are going to use a language called **Visual Basic**. What you will find, regardless of the language you learn first, is that most computer languages have many similar features so once you learn one language, it is very possible to read other languages and much easier to learn how to program using other languages.

To create a program, we need to have a workshop full of tools to help us out. This book is about programming the Visual Basic language and Microsoft, who created Visual Basic, has provided us the workshop and tools to create these programs. The workshop we will use to create our Visual Basic programs is **Visual Studio.Net**. We assume you have Visual Studio.Net already installed on your computer. If you do not, please find out how you can get it installed before you continue on. In addition, we are using Visual Studio.Net 2010 but the same programs we will be creating can be created in other versions of Visual Studio.Net so if you do not have Visual Studio.Net 2010, do not worry, you can still learn Visual Basic using this book with any version of Visual Studio.

Let's get the workshop running. On the bottom left of your computer screen, you should see *start* (e.g.). Click *start*, and then click *All Programs*. In the big list that comes up, find *Microsoft Visual Studio 2010* and move your mouse over top of these words. In the list that displays, find *Microsoft Visual Studio 2010* and click on it.

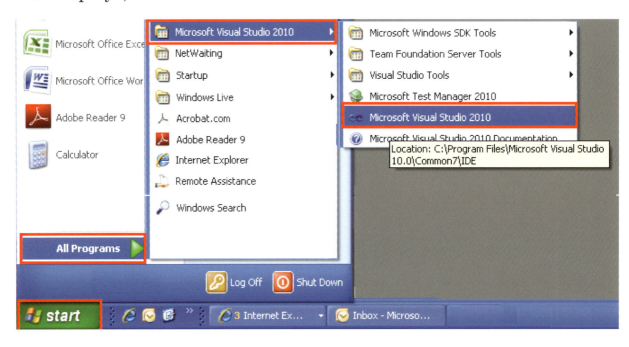

Now the door of your workshop will appear with all kinds of places you can go. The first place we want to go is our Visual Basic workbench so we can start building our program. To get there, in the upper left corner shown below outlined with a red box, we click on *NewProject*. This opens the door to our workshop and lets us in.

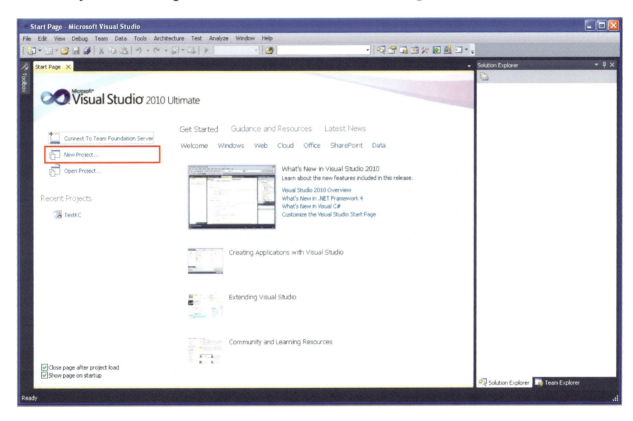

The next screen that pops up is asking us specifically what workbench we want to go to. We want to use the *Visual Basic, Windows Forms Application* workbench or template as indicated with the red boxes below. Find the *Windows Application* under Visual Basic and click it (be careful not to double-click. See Chapter 2 if you double click). You may have to look under Other Languages like shown below depending on how you set up your workbench when you first started it up.

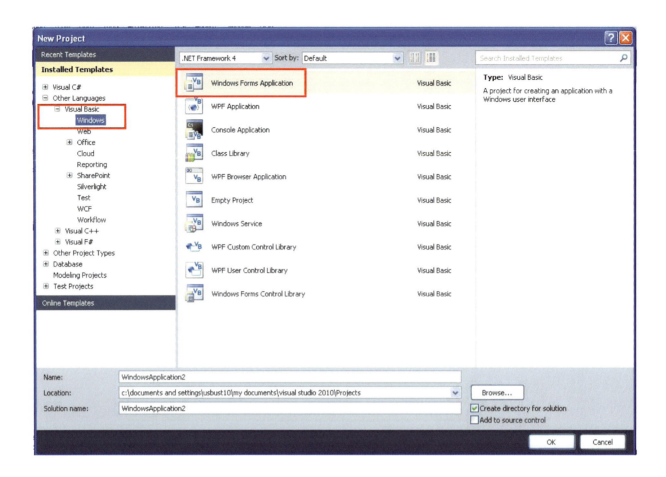

Before we open this workbench and start building our Visual Basic program, we have the opportunity to name our project to whatever we want to call it. Visual Studio gives us a name (example: WindowsApplication2) but you should always make up a name that you can remember and is something that will identify what your program is doing. Please feel free to name this project anything you want to call it but I will name my project "EasyGame". Change the name and click OK as outlined in the red box below.

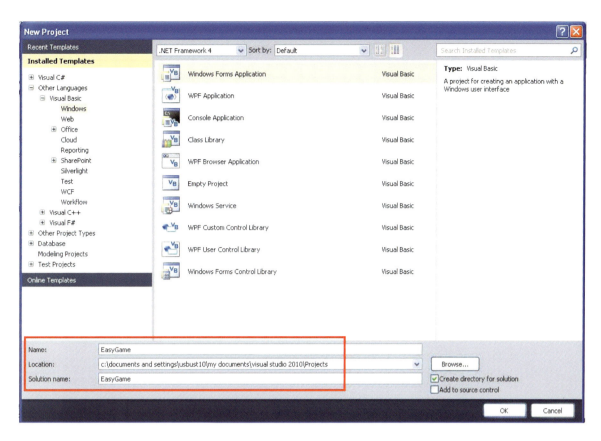

Now we are in our workshop at our workbench and ready to build a program. The workshop should look something like:

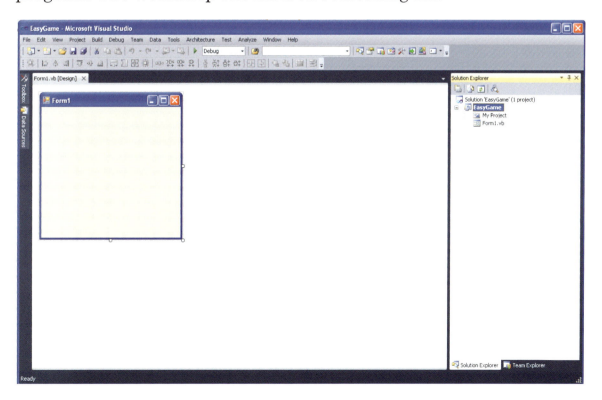

In your workshop, you now have a Form (example: Form1).

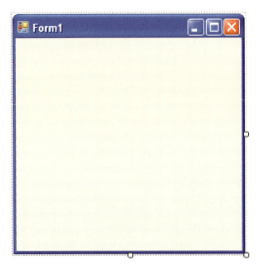

A Form is a surface where you can interact with your program; a window that appears on your computer that lets you play with or use the program you created.

To create some type of interaction with your program, we will need to select some controls. In Visual Basic, controls are things like Text Boxes, Labels, and Buttons. We use controls to create a way to tell the program what we want it to know, and give the program a way to respond back to us. To add a control to your Form, just put your mouse over the Toolbox tab on the upper left hand side. This will open up your toolbox and you can select the controls you want.

 →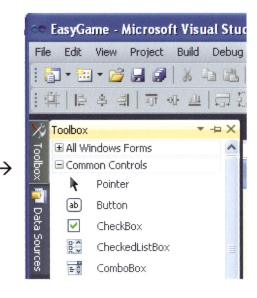

One of the first controls in your toolbox is a Button. Click on Button (ab Button) with your left mouse button, hold your mouse button and drag over to the Form, or click the Button, move the mouse to the form and click on the form where you want to place it. Drag, or Select and Click, both will let you put controls on a form. The difference is that dragging the control to the form shows how the control will align with other controls. Whichever works for you is what you should do but I use the drag and drop method. When you reach your Form while dragging the button, the Toolbox will hide and you will see a little box that tells you the position on your form where the control will be placed. Put this anywhere on the form and release the mouse button and your Button will appear where you placed it.

You should see something like this:

If you do not like where your Button is placed, you can click on to it and drag it to anywhere on your Form (be careful not to double-click it).

Likewise, we can drag and drop other Controls. For our EasyGame, let's drag and drop two Label controls and one Textbox:

A Label and abl TextBox. Drag and drop them like what you see here:

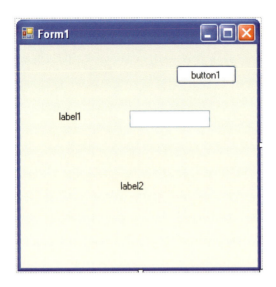

Note that the controls create a name with the Control type (example: label, button) followed by a number starting with one (1) and incrementing by one. You see we have label1 and label2 where each label was named by the system automatically. You cannot name two Controls with the same name; names must always be unique. If we do not like the name of our Control, we can change it using the Properties of the Control. If you click on any Control, there is a Property Manager that displays in the very lower right hand side of our workbench. Click the Button Control (be careful not to double-click) and look at the Property Manager in the lower right:

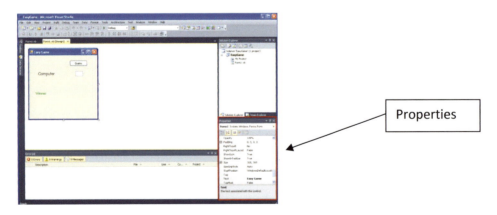

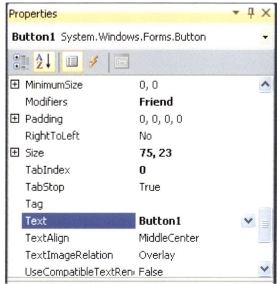

If the Properties window in not displayed like above, click on the View menu item and towards the bottom, click on Properties Window at the bottom like shown here:

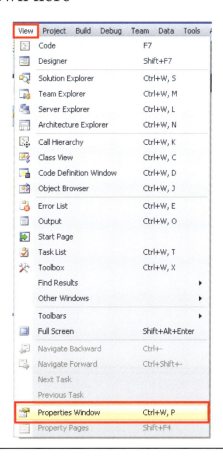

You can see there are a lot of Properties for a Control. There are many of the same properties for all controls as well as many unique properties for each. One of the first properties we see is "Text button1". This is the text that shows in the control itself. Click on where it says button1 and change this to Guess. Notice that the text in your button on your form changes the moment you click on anything else on the screen.

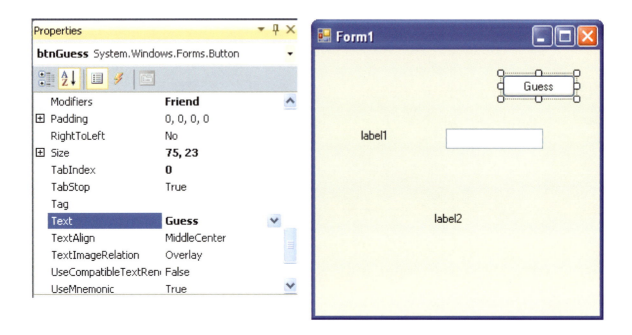

The Button is still named button1 but the text in the button is now Guess. We can see the name of the Button Control by looking under the Properties header.

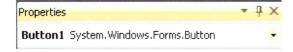

Click on the scroll bar on the very right side of the Properties box and go to the top.

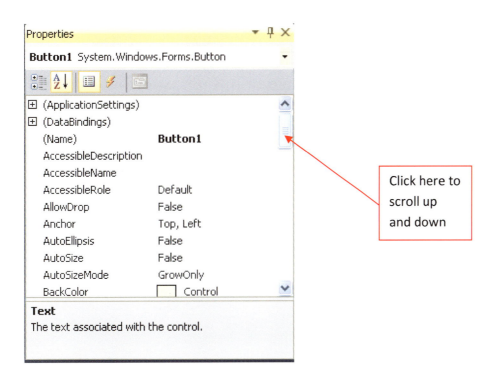

You can now see the Name of the Control as button1. Good programmers, which you are certainly one of, will change the name of the Control to reflect what the Control does. We usually name a control with a three character abbreviation followed by the name we want to give it. In this example, let's rename the control **btnGuess**, where btn is our abbreviation for button and we changed the text to Guess so we can name our control the Guess button or btnGuess.

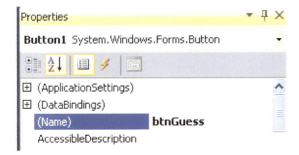

By changing the name, you will not see anything change on your Form but this helps when programming which you will see.

Let's change the names of our Labels and let's change the Font. Click on Label1 (be careful not to double-click). Change the Text to say Computer and let's change the name to lblComputer.

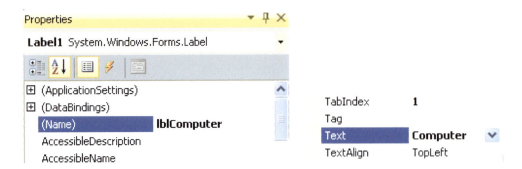

Our Form now looks like:

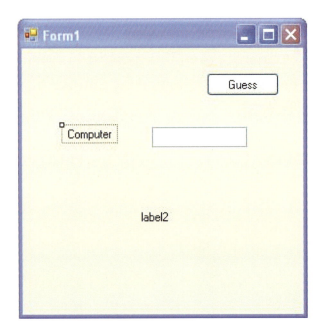

Let's change the Font now. The Font is how the letters look and their size. Under the Properties, if you scroll about half way up, you will see a Property called [+] Font.

Click the little [+] sign and the Font properties will open up.

Here we can change the Size, the type of Font and make it Bold. Let's change the Size to 12 by clicking inside the Size box and typing 12. When you click outside the Size box, you will see your Form change.

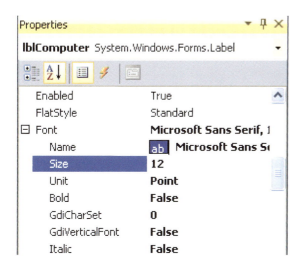
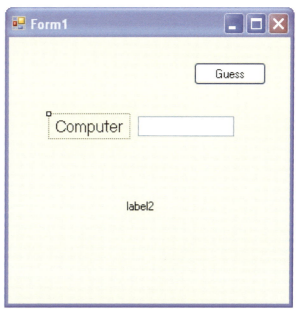

15

Now click on label2. Let's name it lblWinner and change the Text to Winner, change the Font Size to 12 and the ForeColor to Green.

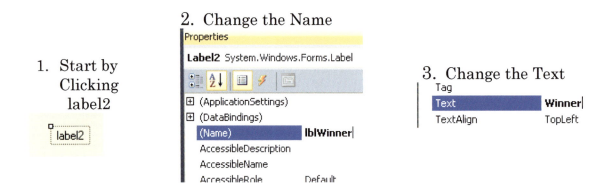

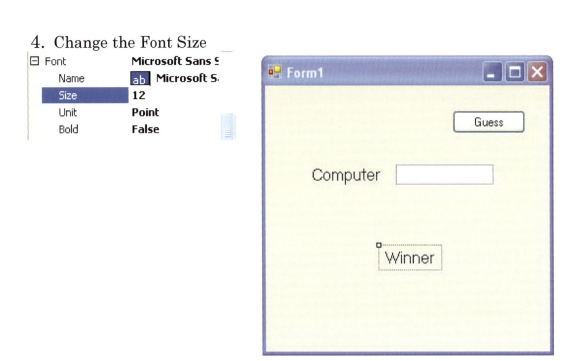

To change the Font Color, change the ForeColor property by clicking the little down arrow.

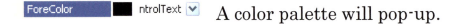 A color palette will pop-up.

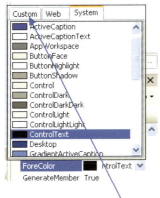

Click the Custom tab at the top and click the Green box. You will see the Property Change.

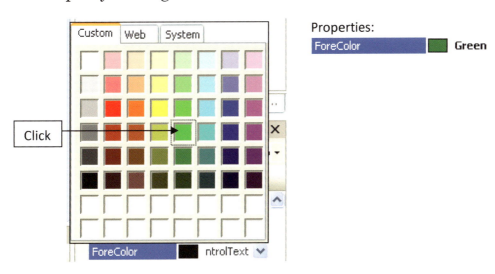

Click

And your Form will now look like:

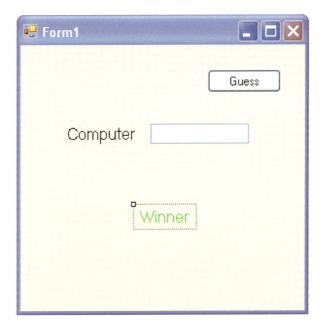

Click on the Textbox (be careful not to double-click) and change the Name to txtMyGuess.

Shorten the width of the Textbox by moving the mouse cursor over the little box on the very left of the textbox, click the left mouse button and then drag the box to the size you want.

Release the Mouse button when you are happy with the size. Make sure the size is big enough to enter a single number between 1 and 9.

Since we only want a number between 1 and 9, let's change one more property on the textbox called MaxLength. Using the scroll bar on the right of the Properties, move it up or down until you see MaxLength:

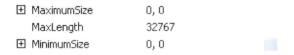

By default, the maximum number of characters you can type into a textbox is 32,767. That's a lot of characters! Let's change this to One

(1) because we only want the user to be able to put in a single digit of either 1, 2, 3, 4, 5, 6, 7, 8, or 9. By changing the MaxLength property to One (1), if the user tries to type "123", this property will let them enter "1" but when they press Two (2), nothing will happen because we have limited the number of characters to just one character.

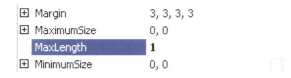

Last, we always want to change the Text property (name) of our Form itself to let the user of our program know what they are running. Click anywhere on the form other than one of the controls (be careful not to double-click). The properties of the form itself will appear in the Properties window on the lower right. Like with other controls (a Form is also a Control), scroll to the Text property and change the name of the Form to "Easy Game."

Now our Form is ready to program. Make sure you save your Project by clicking the Save All icon in the toolbar at the top of your workbench. This will save the work you have done so far and if you exit the workbench (File > Exit), all your hard work will be saved. When you came back to your workbench, you will see your project just like you left it. Get into the habit of saving often by clicking this little button.

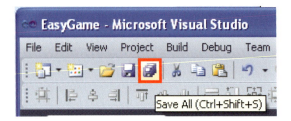

You do not see it, but Microsoft puts a lot of programming in the project before we start coding our program. Before we start coding, let's run what we have. If you press the F5 button at the top of your keyboard, or click the little green arrow in the toolbar, or click the menu item Debug > Start Debugging, all do the same thing and all will start your program.

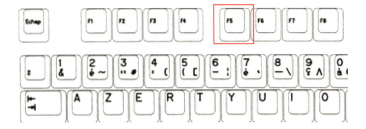

Or

Or

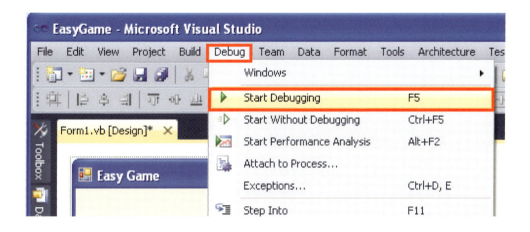

And you will see something like the picture below. You can click the Guess button, put something in the textbox (I put in a 4).

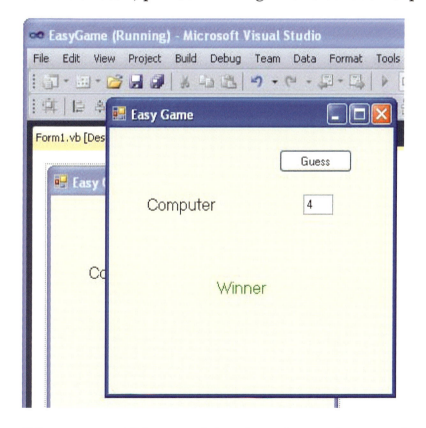

Of course nothing exciting is going to happen because we need to add our own programming or code. To exit your program, click the red X in the upper right side of your Easy Game window and it will stop (not the X of your Workbench, the X in your program window).

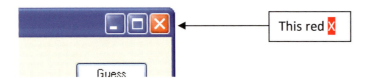

Before we go on to coding your program, I want to add that I encourage any programmer to create a test project and drag and drop the controls under your toolbox onto the Form and then play with the Properties to see what they do and how they change the look of the control on your Form. Each Control has a lot of properties and knowing what they do and how they work can make your programming much more fun.

You have successfully programmed the presentation layer or Client portion of the program. This is the part of the program that the user sees and interacts with. To make this more exciting, we will now turn to how to program or code your application in Chapter 2.

Saving Your Project

You should save your project at this time and often when programming. There is nothing worse than to spend an hour working hard to create a program, loose power, have your programming disappear and then have to start all over again. Save often!

To Save: Click menu items File > Save All (or Ctrl + Shift + S), **or** press the Save All Icon at the top of your screen.

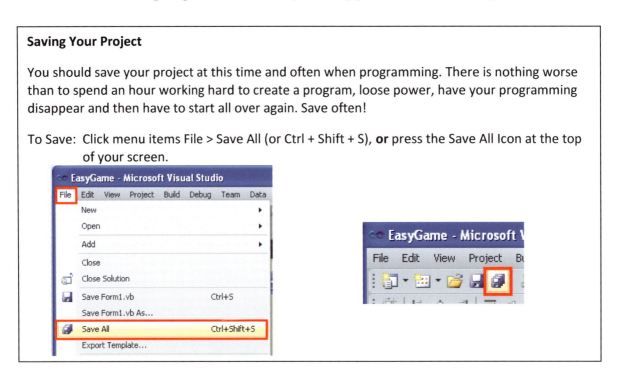

Opening Your Project

Once you save your project, you can exit Visual Studio.Net. When you start Visual Studio.Net again, you will want to open up your project so you can continue to work on it. To open up a saved project, at the Start Page, just click on your project and it will open up, click on the Project Link at the left of this window (Open: Project...), or Click the Menu items File > Open > Project/Solution and find your project on your computer and open the project solution file.

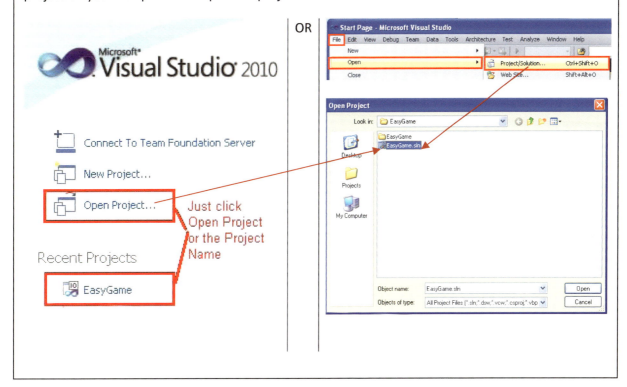

Chapter 1 Definition Review

Program(s)
A computer **program** is a set of instructions that tells a computer how to perform a task.

Statement(s)
A **statement** is a block of code that does something or performs a specific task.

Language
A computer **language** is a set of rules by which we use to create programs.

Visual Basic
Visual Basic is a computer language invented by Microsoft.

Visual Studio.Net
Visual Studio.Net is a work environment created by Microsoft that allows the user to easily write and debug programs .

Template
A **Template** defines the type of programming we want to do.

Form
A **Form** is a customizable area that is used to setup the various controls so a user can interact with the program.

Control
A **Control** is a component that adds special functionality which allows the user of a program to display information or give information to the program. Examples are Buttons, Textboxes and Labels.

Properties
A **Property** is an attribute of a control that allows the programmer to change a Control's name, how a control looks, and how it behaves. Examples are Name, MaxLength, Font Size, and Text.

2. The Code Behind

Now the hard work begins. Not so much because it's really hard but it is less visual and more just writing sentences we call statements as well as memorizing how to do it. Think of the first part we did when we created the Form as a picture to a book report and now we have to write out what the book is about. Drawing a picture is usually much more fun that writing out the story. However, to make our program do the cool things we want it to do, we have to write the story behind the picture.

In Visual Studio.Net, we have the Client or Presentation part of the program, which you have already programmed, and behind that is the code. When a user clicks on the button on our EasyGame program, we want to write some code that tells the program what to do when that button is clicked.

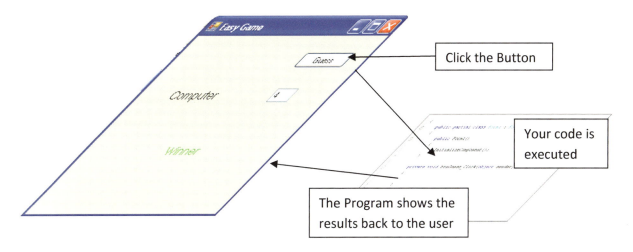

Remember in Chapter 1 when I kept noting to be careful not to double-click, well now I want you to double click. Double-Click anywhere on the form but not on a Control (not on a Label, Textbox or Button). This will open the code portion of your Workbench. You should see something like:

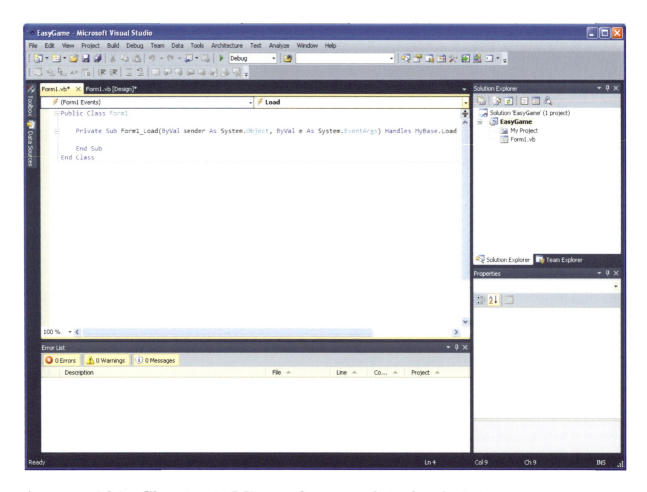

As we said in Chapter 1, Microsoft puts a lot of code into our application already so we do not have to worry about it. Above we see some of that code.

Toggling between your Form and your Code

Like most things on your workbench, we have several ways to do the same thing. Now that you are at the code level, how do you get back to your Form if you wanted to make a change? There are at least three ways to do this:

Use the Tabs at the top of the main window.

Clicking Form1.vb[Design] will take you back to the Form. Clicking Form1.vb will take you to the code.

Or

Click the menu item View and at the very top are the options Code and Designer. Click Code to see the Code and Designer to see your Form.

Or

Above the Properties window on the very right, there is the Solutions Explorer.

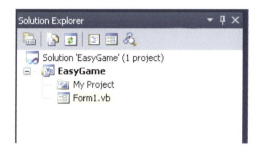

Right click the Form1.vb and you will see the options View Code and View Designer. Choose the one you want to toggle to between your Form and Code.

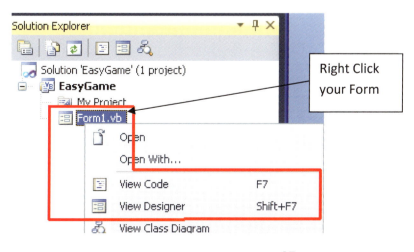

The three ways above will let you move easily between your Code and your Form.

The basic parts of Code is broken down into boxes that go inside one another. The boxes have names like **Namespace**, **Classes** and **Methods**. Classes are boxes in Namespaces and Methods are boxes that are inside a Class.

We will be working with Methods. Methods are the means to solve a task; i.e. "there is a *method* to making this task work". When you click the button on your form, you can create a Method to tell the computer what you want to happen next. Likewise, when your program starts up, there is a Method to tell the program what to do when it starts. We can see this in the Method that was provided when we double-clicked on our form:

```
Private Sub Form1_Load(ByVal sender As System.Object, ByVal e As System.EventArgs) Handles MyBase.Load

End Sub
```

This Method is named Form1_Load and just like the name says, whatever we tell the computer to do when we start our Form, is what happens in this Method.

If you haven't guessed yet, our Easy Game program is a guessing game. You enter a number between 1 and 9 and when you click the Guess button, the computer tells you the number it was thinking of and you will see if you guessed the same number or not.

On the Form we have a label called lblWinner but we do not want to tell the user that they are a winner before they have had a chance to play so when we start our program, we want to hide this label until the user can play the game. To do this, when the program starts, we tell the computer to make this Control (Label) invisible. To do this, we use a statement, or line of code like this:

```vb
Private Sub Form1_Load(ByVal sender As System.Object, ByVal e As System.EventArgs) Handles MyBase.Load
    lblWinner.Visible = False
End Sub
```

The line of code we typed, `lblWinner.Visible = False` tells your label, lblWinner, to be invisible when your program starts. Visible = True means you are visible. Visible = False means you are not visible or you are invisible.

We can also add **comments** to our program. Comments are messages we put into our code to explain what and/or why we did something. This is very helpful when you go back to your program later or if someone else has to look at your program. Sometimes what we do and why we did it is not obvious so we add a comment to explain the purpose of the statement or a set of statements to make our program easier to understand. Comments are denoted by putting a single quote (or apostrophe) anywhere in the program:

```vb
' This is a comment
```

The important thing about comments is that the program just ignores them so you can type anything you want after the single quote (') . You should get into the habit of putting comments in to your code to give you a more clear explanation of what your code is doing.

```vb
Private Sub Form1_Load(ByVal sender As System.Object, ByVal e As System.EventArgs)
    ' Turn the Label Invisible
    lblWinner.Visible = False
End Sub
```

Now let's make the button do something. To create the Method for your button, go back to the form in design mode and double-click the button with your left mouse button. We will see the resulting code created by Microsoft to look like:

```vbnet
Private Sub btnGuess_Click(ByVal sender As System.Object, ByVal e As System.EventArgs) Handles …

End Sub
```

This is what we want which is a button click or in our case, btnGuess_Click. By now, you can see that our Methods begin with the name we have given our Control followed by an underscore, "_", followed by a verb of what we want to do. We want to do the Click Method when we click the btnGuess button.

When we click the Guess button, we want to generate a number and compare that number to the number we entered. If the computer generated number is the same as the number we entered, then we are declared a Winner. If it is not the same number, then we are a Loser.

The first thing we want to do when we click the Guess button is to check if the user entered a number. If the user did not enter a number then there is nothing to guess. To check this, we use an IF ... THEN statement. In simple terms, the IF statement looks like:

    IF something is what we want THEN do something

OR

    IF something is NOT what we want, THEN do something

We want to create an IF statement that says if the number entered in our textbox called txtMyGuess is not a number between 1 and 9, we want to stop and tell the user that they must enter a number between 1 and 9. We do this with a few IF statements.

First we can check to see if something was entered at all; in other words. if no one entered anything in our txtMyGuess textbox, we want to let them know they must enter a number between 1 and 9.

Type the code below just as you see it, in between the curly brackets of your btnGuess_click Method as in the red box below:

```
Private Sub btnGuess_Click(ByVal sender As System.Object, ByVal e As ...
    If txtMyGuess.Text = "" Then
        lblWinner.Visible = True
        lblWinner.Text = "You must enter a number between 1 and 9"
        lblWinner.ForeColor = Color.Red
        Return
    End If
End Sub
```

In the code above, if our textbox called txtMyGuess is equal to nothing `txtMyGuess.Text = ""` then

Make the label **lblWinner** visible: `lblWinner.Visible = True`

Put the error text into the label: `lblWinner.Text = "You must enter a number between 1 and 9"`

Turn the letters Red: `lblWinner.ForeColor = Color.Red`

And return the user back to the form: `Return`

Last, note that the IF statement ends with End If to tell the program that there are no more statements contained in this IF statement.

Let me take a moment to mention an important concept that as you were writing the code, you would have seen and that is Intellisense. As you write the code, Visual Studio gives you options. When you write lblWinner and type period (.), you will get a drop down list of all the properties you can program with lblWinner. In fact, when you start to write "lbl", you will see everything that begins with lbl and you can choose the item you want by either clicking on it or pressing <tab> and Visual Studio will complete the name for you. I encourage you to use Intellisense because it keeps you honest in that you do not have to worry about capital or lower case letters, or if you correctly spelled the name. Below, I type "lblC" and it shows me the name of the control I want to add. I can click it or press tab to have it on the program:

Run the program now (press F5) and just click the Guess button.

If an Error is in your program

If you see this screen pop up:

This means that there is an error in your program. Click No and look for the error. The Error will be highlight with a Red Squiggly line below the statement that made the error like in this example:

```
If txtMyGuess.Text = "" Then
    lblWinner.Visibl = True
    lblWinner.Text = "You must enter a number between 1 and 9"
    lblWinner.ForeColor = Color.Red
    Return
End If
```

In the code above, I left off the "e" at the end of Visible and thus the system does not know what I mean. If I add the "e", the program will run because there are no errors.

Running the program and pressing the Guess button will give a result something like:

Obviously looking at this, we can see our error message runs off the end of the page. We can fix this a couple of ways: we can move the label and/or change the font size. Let's move the label first and see if that fixes things. Click the Red X on the form to stop your program.

To move the label, click on the label and drag to the left, close to the side of the form:

When we run our program (press F5), and click Guess without entering a number, we now see:

Our error message is getting cutoff on the end. We can make the font smaller or fix the size of the label. Let's try and make the font size one size smaller. Stop the program by clicking the Red X. From the

Form in Designer mode, click the label lblWinner and go to the right to the Properties box. Find Font, click the little [+] in front of Font and expand out the Font properties. Change the size from 12 to 10:

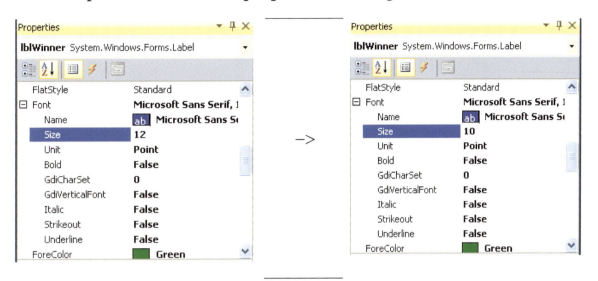

Now run your EasyGame program, click F5, click the Guess button and we see:

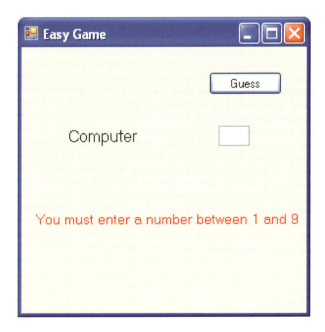

Yea! Our error message fits on our form.

The process you just went through is called **debugging** your program or getting the bugs out. Debugging a program is often the process of testing something in your program, seeing how the program works and if you do not like the way it looks or the results, you change your program until you get the desired results. You have just debugged your first program.

We have fixed the label lblWinner to properly display our error message and we have entered the code that checks if the user has left our textbox blank, now let's check if the user entered a number. Go back to the program code and enter the following code under the previous IF code as in the red box below.

```vb
Private Sub btnGuess_Click(ByVal sender As System.Object, ByVal e As …
    ' Check to see if the user put something into the Guess box
    If txtMyGuess.Text = "" Then
        lblWinner.Visible = True
        lblWinner.Text = "You must enter a number between 1 and 9"
        lblWinner.ForeColor = Color.Red
        Return
    End If
    ' Look at the character entered and make sure it is a number
    If IsNumeric(txtMyGuess.Text) = False Then
        lblWinner.Visible = True
        lblWinner.Text = "You must enter a number between 1 and 9"
        lblWinner.ForeColor = Color.Red
        Return
    End If
End Sub
```

We need to use the built-in system character function IsNumeric. This will tell the program what the user entered is a number or not. The code `IsNumeric(txtMyGuess.Text)` lets us know if the entry in the Textbox is a number (True) or not (False). We are asking if the IsNumeric is False (`If IsNumeric(txtMyGuess.Text) = False Then`) because if it is false, or not true, then we know something other than a number was entered.

Textboxes are be default, a string variable which is a set of characters. To be clear, a string is numeric when it has all numbers (example "0123456789"), it is alpha (example "abcdef") when it is all letters, or it is comprised of special character (example "?><!@#$%").

If the IsNumeric is false, `= False`, then we know the user entered something other than a number and we can report the error and exit the button click Method to tell the User they need to enter a number between 1 and 9.

```
lblWinner.Visible = True
lblWinner.Text = "You must enter a number between 1 and 9"
lblWinner.ForeColor = Color.Red
Return
```

That's about all we need to do to make sure the user enters a number. If we do not do these steps, our program will error out and/or not work properly if a user enters something other than a number. It is important, no matter how tedious, to make sure the user enters a proper value.

Since this is a guessing game, the computer must create a number and then match that number against the number we entered and if they are the same, we win! If they are not the same, we lose. To get the computer to create a number, we use a built-in Random function. To use a Random number, a number created by the computer and is different every time, we ask the computer to give us a number, we declare a variable **rNum** as Random:

```
Dim rNum As Random = New Random()
```

This may seem a little redundant but again, computers aren't very smart so in this case we are telling the computer we want a variable named rNum, it's random and uses the Random function. If you were a computer and wanted a nose to smell, you would have to tell yourself that you have a nose that is a nose. This may seem silly but in order to create a random number we must tell the computer we have a random variable that is random. This is called **instantiation**.

After we tell the computer we have the random variable rNum, we can use it to generate a number and we want to put that number into an integer variable; an integer is any whole number like -2, 0, 1, 2, 14, ... and not 2.5 or 203.333. We declare an Integer variable and tell our Random function that we want the number between 1 and 9. By default, the Random number generator, creates Integer numbers so we are good to go with the code above. To get our number between 1 and 9, we tell the Random function to give us such a number with the following code:

```
Dim intNum As Integer = rNum.Next(1, 10)
```

In the code above, we tell the computer we want to get the next "random" number that is not less than one but less than 10 (in other words, between 1 and 9), `rNum.Next(1, 10)`. `rNum.Next(1, 10)` will generate a number between 1 and what is less than 10, or 9. Having number 10 and meaning a number less than 10 can be a little confusing but this is how Visual Basic works so we must just remember this as the way the random function interprets what we give it. If our code was `Random(1, 9)`, then we would get a number between 1 and 8.

In addition, note that I named my Integer variable intNum. It is good practice to start a variable name with the type of variable it is. "int" stands for Integer, "str" for String, and so on.

We have a number we entered and we have a number the computer created so all we have left to do is to see if our number and the computer's number are the same.

Before however, we need to do a little housecleaning to let the users see the results. Let's have the computer tell us what number it created. Type this statement next:

```
lblComputer.Text = "Computer says: " + intNum.ToString
```

We use our label lblComputer and place into that label a note that lets the user know this is from the computer, `"Computer says: "`, and then we add to the sentence the number the computer created, `intNum.ToString`. Since Labels are also string types, we convert the number intNum to a string with an easy to use, built-in system function called "ToString".

Next, we have to tell the computer to show the label that lets us know if we won or lost:

```
lblWinner.Visible = True
```

And finally we use an IF ... THEN ... ELSE statement to check to see if our number is the same as the computer created number, and if it is true, we win, if not (Else), we lose.

```
If intNum = CInt(txtMyGuess.Text) Then
    lblWinner.Text = "YOU ARE A WINNER"
    lblWinner.ForeColor = Color.Green
Else
    lblWinner.Text = "Sorry, you lost"
    lblWinner.ForeColor = Color.DarkBlue
End If
```

Looking at this a little closer, the first line we are comparing the number generated by the computer (intNum) to the number the user entered (txtMyGuess.Text). However, since the number generated by the computer is a number and the number entered by the user is in text (string) format, we have to convert the text to a number before we compare the two numbers. In other words, we cannot compare a number to text, we must first convert the text to a number and then compare the two numbers. Even if it looks like we have two numbers, they must be the same type before we can compare. Imagine if you had two cookies on the table. They may look the same and you bite into one of the cookies and it is soft and tastes really good. You bite into the second cookie and it is plastic so you cannot eat it. Both cookies look alike but one is real and the other is plastic. In order to compare the taste of both cookies, we have to convert the plastic cookie into a real cookie, then we can taste it and say whether it is good or not. In the same way, in order to compare anything in Visual Basic programming, we must make sure both objects we are comparing are the same type.

We use the System function conversion to Integer to make our textbox string into a number:

```
CInt(txtMyGuess.Text)
```

So `If intNum = CInt(txtMyGuess.Text) Then`, or if the computer number is the same (=) as we entered, then we tell the user that they are a winner by changing the text in our lblWinner label to say the user is a winner and changing the color to green to make it easy to see we are a winner:

```
lblWinner.Text = "YOU ARE A WINNER"
lblWinner.ForeColor = Color.Green
```

If we did not win, or the numbers were not the same, then we lost. We use the ELSE to determine the fact that we did not win and we tell the user they lost.

```
else ' else you lost
    lblWinner.Text = "Sorry, you lost"
    lblWinner.ForeColor = Color.DarkBlue
```

We do this by putting in the lblWinner label that the user lost and changing the color to dark blue. The color does not matter but we make it different so it's easy to see if we won or lost.

The entire code for our button should look like

```
Private Sub btnGuess_Click(ByVal sender As System.Object, ByVal e As System.EventArgs) Handles btnGuess.Click
    ' Check to see if the user put something into the Guess box
    If txtMyGuess.Text = "" Then
        lblWinner.Visible = True
        lblWinner.Text = "You must enter a number between 1 and 9"
        lblWinner.ForeColor = Color.Red
        Return
    End If
    ' Look at the character entered and make sure it is a number
    If IsNumeric(txtMyGuess.Text) = False Then
        lblWinner.Visible = True
        lblWinner.Text = "You must enter a number between 1 and 9"
        lblWinner.ForeColor = Color.Red
        Return
    End If
    ' Instantiate a new random number
    Dim rNum As Random = New Random()
    ' Declare and get a Random number between 1 and 9 (<10)
    Dim intNum As Integer = rNum.Next(1, 10)
```

```vbnet
    ' Show what the computer came up with
    lblComputer.Text = "Computer says: " + intNum.ToString
    ' Make the Winner label visible
    lblWinner.Visible = True
    ' if the num the computer came up with and your number match,
    ' then you are a winner
    If intNum = CInt(txtMyGuess.Text) Then
        lblWinner.Text = "YOU ARE A WINNER"
        lblWinner.ForeColor = Color.Green
    Else ' else you lost
        lblWinner.Text = "Sorry, you lost"
        lblWinner.ForeColor = Color.DarkBlue
    End If
End Sub
```

Now you are ready to play. You have written a program that checks to see if what the user entered is a number, the computer creates a number and you compare the number generated by the computer to the number entered by the user and if they are equal, you declare the user a winner, if they are not equal, you tell the user they lost.

Run by pressing F5, or by clicking the Debug menu item and then clicking Start Debugging, or by just clicking the little green arrow. You will see:

Enter a number in the textbox:

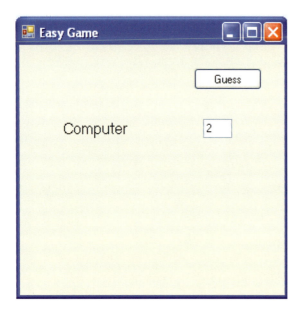

Click Guess:

You see what the Computer guessed (3) and that you lost. Click Guess again and again. You will see the Computer number change and if you continue to click, very soon, you will see:

YOU ARE A WINNER!!! because you have written your first program using Visual Basic.

> More Fun!
>
> **Here are some suggestions to enhance your program. Try these and figure out how to program:**
>
> - How would you test for a number between 1 and 99?
>
> - How would you use a range to tell the user if they were close; example, if you were guessing a number between 1 and 99 and you were within 10 numbers to the guess, you could tell the user they were close to being a winner.

Chapter 2 Definition Review

Namespace, Classes and Methods
A .Net program is structured into three basic components: **Methods** are contained within **Classes** and Classes are contained within **Namespaces**.

Comments
Comments are designated by putting a single quote (or an apostrophe) and then whatever you want to write, example: ' this is a comment. Use comments in your program to tell yourself and other programmers what the code is doing.

Debug
When you **debug** a program you are writing code, testing the code, changing the code, testing again, over and over again until your program is what you want it to be.

Function
A **function** is a Method you call that returns a value. Built-in functions are Methods provided within Visual Basic that you can use to do common things like convert data types.

IF ... THEN ... ELSE
IF ... THEN ... ELSE allows the programmer to check for conditions and if the condition is true, then execute the code that is written for the true condition, if false, then execute the code after the ELSE. You do not have to have an ELSE statement, it is optional. A IF statement ends with END IF.

Variables
A **variable** is a container in which to store information in program (running) memory. Variables can be of many types described below. Variables cannot by default intermingle so that a string variable cannot be assigned to an integer variable.

Data Types

Below is a table of the different Data Types in Visual Basic courtesy of Microsoft at http://msdn.microsoft.com/en-us/library/47zceaw7(VS.71).aspx

Visual Basic type	Value range
Boolean	**True** or **False**.
Byte	0 through 255 (unsigned).
Char	0 through 65535 (unsigned).
Date	0:00:00 on January 1, 0001 through 11:59:59 PM on December 31, 9999.
Decimal	0 through +/-79,228,162,514,264,337,593,543,950,335 with no decimal point; 0 through +/-7.9228162514264337593543950335 with 28 places to the right of the decimal; smallest nonzero number is +/-0.0000000000000000000000000001 (+/-1E-28).
Double (double-precision floating-point)	-1.79769313486231570E+308 through -4.94065645841246544E-324 for negative values; 4.94065645841246544E-324 through 1.79769313486231570E+308 for positive values.
Integer	-2,147,483,648 through 2,147,483,647.
Long (long integer)	-9,223,372,036,854,775,808 through 9,223,372,036,854,775,807.
Object	Any type can be stored in a variable of type **Object**.
Short	-32,768 through 32,767.
Single (single-precision floating-point)	-3.4028235E+38 through -1.401298E-45 for negative values; 1.401298E-45 through 3.4028235E+38 for positive values.
String (variable-length)	0 to approximately 2 billion Unicode characters.
User-Defined Type (structure)	Each member of the structure has a range determined by its data type and independent of the ranges of the other members.

3. Hangman

Now that you have learned programming basics, we can start to create more fun programs. The next program we will create is the classic Hangman game. In this game, the user of the program will guess a word by entering each letter, one at a time. If the letter is part of the word they are safe. If the letter is not part of the word they are trying to guess, a part of the person being hanged is drawn on the form. When the entire figure of a person is drawn before the word is guessed, you lose. If you guess the word before the figure of a person is completely drawn on the form, you win!

Like in our first program, we need to create the project and create the form. Startup Visual Studio.Net, and create a new project named Hangman:

1) Click New Project ...

Make sure your project type is Visual Basic > Windows, select the Windows Forms Application template and name your project *Hangman*, then click OK.

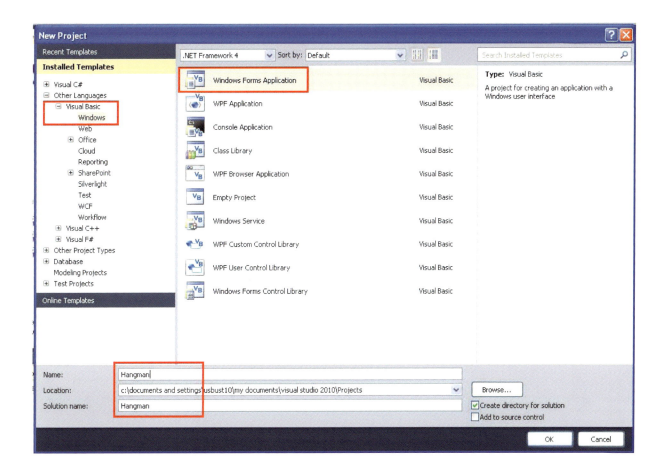

You should see something familiar like:

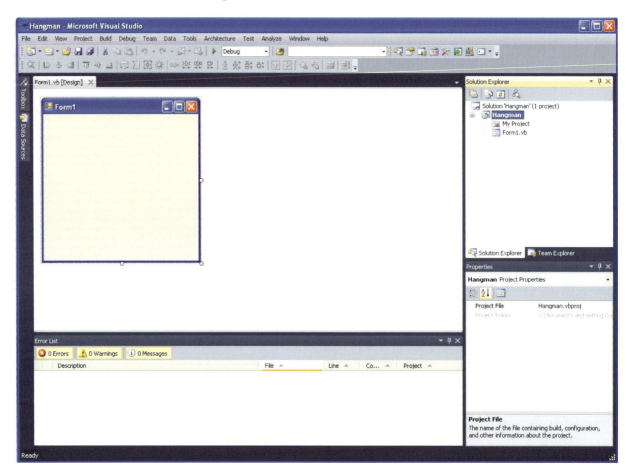

Your project is ready to begin programming. Click on the Form and change the Form Text property to Hangman:

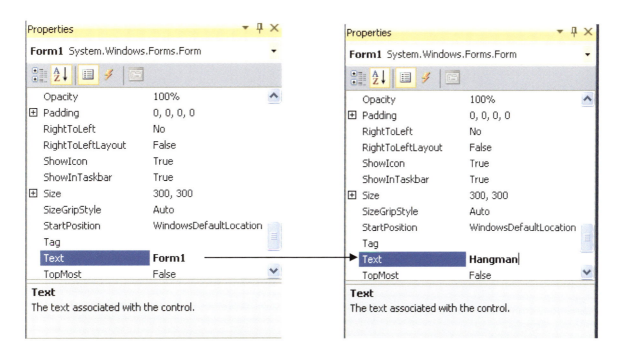

Place two (2) buttons on the form (remember Toolbox, Button):

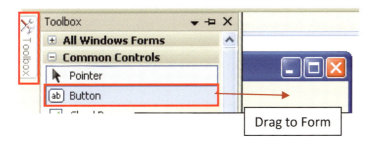

So you end up with something that looks like:

Change the name in Properties of button1 to btnGetWord:

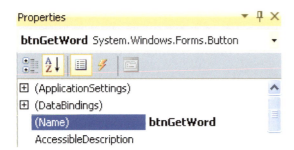

Change the Text in Properties of btnGetWord to "Get Word":

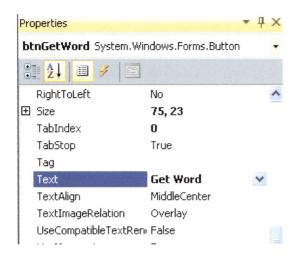

So it looks like:

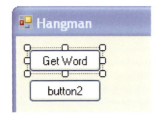

Change the name in Properties of button2 to btnGuess:

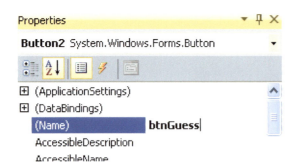

Change the Text in Properties of btnGuess to "Guess":

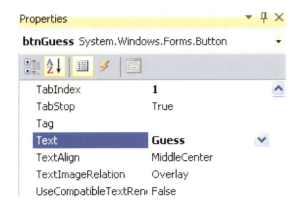

So it looks like:

Add a textbox from your Toolbox to the Form next to btnGuess:

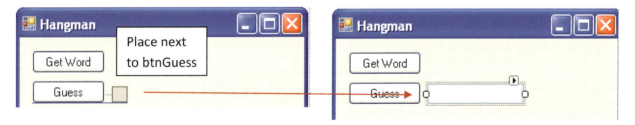

Shorten the size to about One character:

Change the name of the textbox to txtGuess and MaxLength to "1":

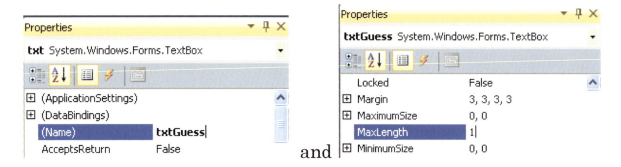

Now we have a button to get a word so we can guess, and a button and textbox that we can enter a letter and click Guess to see if it's part of the word we have gotten.

We are going to be guessing 5 letter words so we need to create 5 labels, each label we represent a letter in our word. This can be a little tricky to visualize because when you drag a label from your toolbox to your form it has a default size much bigger than what we need and if you try to put all 5 at one time, they could overlap each other and make it hard to resize. To make this easy, do one label at a time, starting from the left of your form, and resizing each label before dragging another label to your form. With Labels, the way to resize is by entering a character into the Text property. In our case, we will replace the Text "label1" with an underscore character "_".

Drag label1 and drop it like shown below:

Now change the name of this Label to lblLet1 and the Text property to "_".

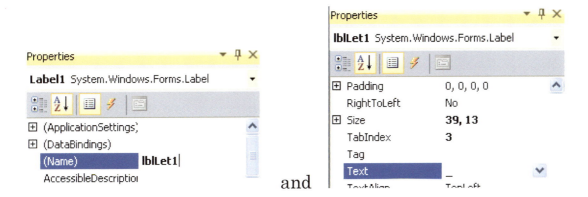
and

So now our label on the Form looks like:

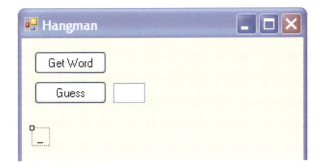

Do the next label near the first and just to the right:

Change the name of this label to lblLet2 and change the Text to "_":

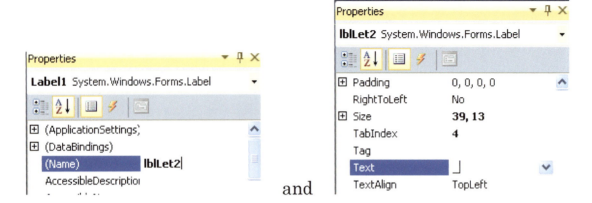 and

So our Form now looks like:

We are going to add Three more labels just to the right of this label, one at a time, changing their names to lblLet3, lblLet4 and lblLet5, and changing the Text property to be "_":

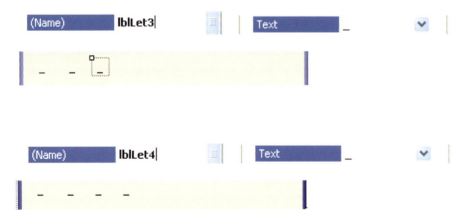

After you are done, the Form should look something like:

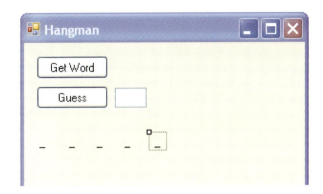

Next is the Man. To draw the man, we will use Three labels: the Head, Body and Legs. Lets add the Head first. Drag a label to your form about center below your letter labels. Once that is done, your Form should look like:

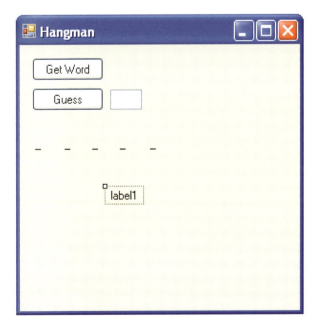

Change the label Name property to lblHead and change the Text property to a capital O.

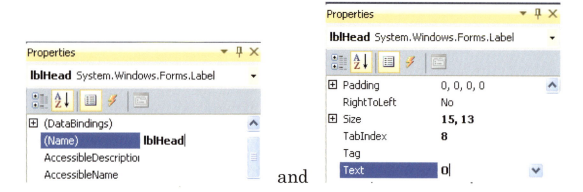
and

Your Form should look like:

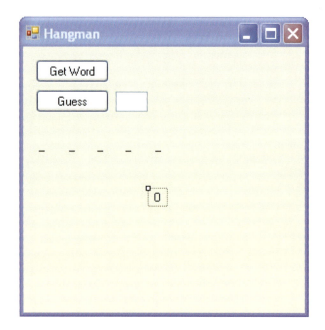

Next is the Body. This will be a little trickier because we want to align the Body label under the lblHead. Drag a label and place it under lblHead that you just created.

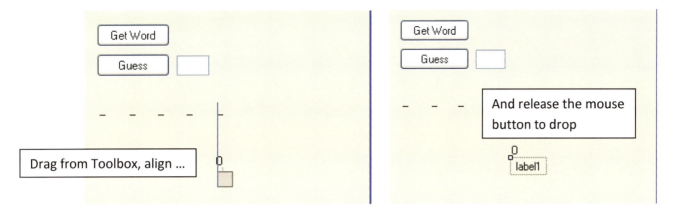

Change the Name property to lblBody and in the Text property enter forward slash, bar, back slash ("/|\").

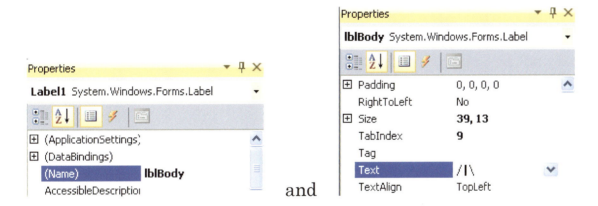

and

If you were lucky, your Body aligns right beneath the Head. If you were not lucky, you might see something like:

To align the lblBody to lblHead, use your arrow keys on your keyboard and move the lblBody in the direction it needs to go.

In my case, I will use the left arrow to align the body under the head. If you need to, click the lblBody label in order to put the focus on the label you want to move. After you use the keyboard arrows, the Form should look like:

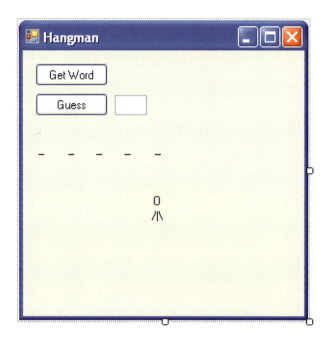

Next we add the legs. Drag another label and place underneath lblBody. Name this label lblLegs and in the Text property, enter forward-slash, back slash ("/\"):

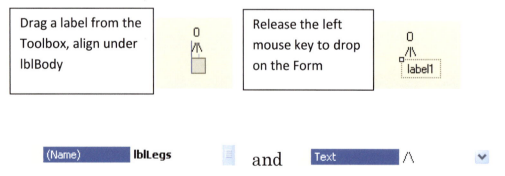

Your form might look like:

Use the arrow keys to align so your Form will look like:

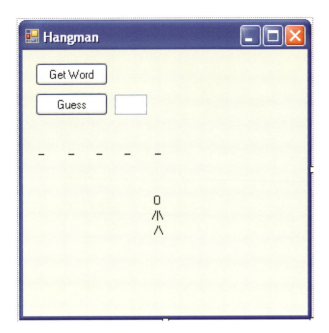

If you would like, you can use other labels and use the Text property to make a gallows. This is not necessary but would make the screen look more like the classic game. You do not have to name these labels unless you wish; just change the Text property for the effect.

I did mine like this:

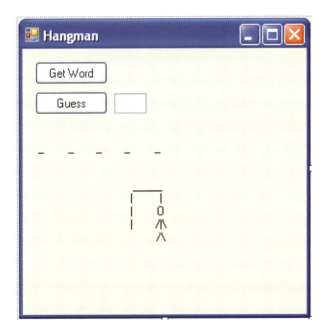

To create my gallows, I used 5 more labels, one for each vertical line and one for the lines across the top where I enter several underscores to give the look of a line ("____"). Again, this is not necessary but I encourage you to play with this if you feel you are ready to try.

Last, let's add a Message label so we can give the user messages. At the bottom of the screen, drag a label from your toolbox and drop it on the Form in the lower left. Change the Name property to lblMessage and change the Text property to Message.

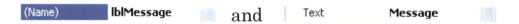

So your completed form should look like:

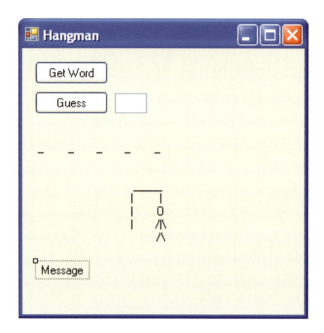

Remember to Save! =

The Code Behind

We have created our Form and all the controls we need to create our game. Now it is time to create the code. Double-click on the form but not on a Control. This will take you to the code page and you should see:

```vb
Private Sub Form1_Load(ByVal sender As System.Object, ByVal e As System.EventArgs) Handles MyBase.Load

End Sub
```

Like with our first program, we want to turn things off and change some properties to start. Since we have not guessed yet, we will not want to see the "man"; therefore, we will make the necessary labels invisible.

```vb
lblHead.Visible = False
lblBody.Visible = False
lblLegs.Visible = False
```

Since we do not have a Word yet to guess, we want to disable the btnGuess button and the txtGuess textbox. Therefore, our Form_Load method will look like:

```vb
Private Sub Form1_Load(ByVal sender As System.Object, ByVal e As System.EventArgs) …
    lblHead.Visible = False
    lblBody.Visible = False
    lblLegs.Visible = False
    btnGuess.Enabled = False
    txtGuess.Enabled = False
End Sub
```

When you set a control "Enabled = false", the control is still visible on the screen but you cannot do anything with the control. In our case, we cannot click the button or enter anything into the textbox.

Recap:
Visible property = changes whether a control is visible or not on the Form.

Enabled property = changes whether a control is useable or not.

Remember how to run your program?

Press F5   or   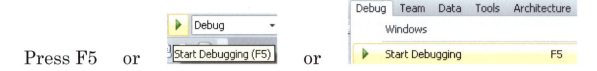   or

If we run the program, we will see:

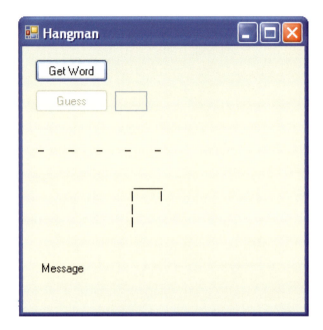

The btnGuess is still visible as you can see but not useable. Same with txtGuess. The labels that make up the "man" are not visible.

Click the Red X on the upper right to exit your program.

Back on the Form, double-click the Get Word button, btnGetWord.

The resulting code will be;

```
Private Sub btnGetWord_Click(ByVal sender As System.Object, ByVal e As …

End Sub
```

In this Method, we want to select a word to guess. There are probably several ways to do this but we will use an Array and then randomly pick a word from the Array. An Array is a variable that has multiple compartments that can hold data. Think of a variable as a box and an Array as a chest of drawers. You can put your shirts or your socks in the box, but not both at the same time. With a chest of drawers (an Array), you can put your shirts in one drawer and your socks in another drawer. We have seen a single variable that contains one thing. As an example, we can declare a string variable like:

    Dim strWord As String = "hello"

strWord has one and only one set of characters or word. We can use a string Array to use the same variable name but have many words stored in it:

    Dim strWord() As String = {"hello", "goodbye", "I am here"}

We reference which string or word we want to use by the number (ordinal) of the compartment:

    strGetWord = strWord(2)

With Visual Basic, all Arrays start at position Zero (0). Therefore, using the sample above

    strWord(0) is going to be "hello"

    strWord(1) is going to be "goodbye"

    strWord(2) is going to be "I am here"

and just so you know, strWord(3) will throw an exception and cause your program to error because nothing exists in strWord(3).

We can create an Array to store the words we want to guess in our Hangman game:

```
Dim strWords() as String = {"SHARP", "WORDS", "MICRO", "BRAIN", "GRAPE"}
```

Note: you can use any 5 letter words you wish. Just make sure they do not have repeating letters; example, a bad word would be APPLE because it has two Ps.

Please note that the words we are putting into our array are marked by Curly Brackets { ... }; whereas our postion within the array is marked by parenthesis (...).

Using our str*Words* Array above, we would have:

strWords(0) is "SHARP"

strWords(1) is "WORDS"

strWords(2) is "MICRO"

strWords(3) is "BRAIN"

strWords(4) is "GRAPE"

To borrow from our first program, we can create a Random number between 0 and 4, and use that number to choose a word from our words Array.

```vb
' We declare an Array with 5 different 5 character words
Dim strWords() As String = {"SHARP", "WORDS", "MICRO", "BRAIN", "GRAPE"}
' Instantiate a new random number
Dim rNum As Random = New Random()
' Declare and get a Random number between 0 and 4 (<5)
Dim intNum As Integer = rNum.Next(0, 5)
' Randomly choose a word to guess
strWord2Guess = strWords(intNum)
```

Wait, where did strWord2Guess come from? Because we need to use the word we have chosen when we guess the letters, we declare the string variable strWord2Guess as what is called in class. This allows the variable to be used in any of our Methods, and will store and keep whatever we put there so that if one Method places some data into the In Class variable, when another Method looks at it, that information will be there. To use In Class variables, we must declare them at the top, right under our Class definition. Go to the very top of your code page and type the following after your class statement like so:

```vb
    Public Class Form1
Type here → Public strWord2Guess As String ← Type here
```

Add two more declarations while you are there and we will use these later as outlined in the box below.

```vbnet
Public Class Form1
    ' Add these three variables for use througout the class
    Public strWord2Guess As String
    Public intHangLocation As Integer
    Public intWordLetters As Integer
```

So now when we type:

```vbnet
    ' Randomly choose a word to guess
    strWord2Guess = strWords(intNum)
```

strWord2Guess is a declared variable and we will not get an error.

We have the word we are going to guess at this point but we need to add under the `btnGetWord_Click` Method some additional housecleaning items. Type the following after `strWord2Guess = strWords(intNum)` (read the comments to understand the purpose of the code)

```vbnet
    ' Make our Guess controls useable since we now have a word
    btnGuess.Enabled = True
    txtGuess.Enabled = True
    ' Disable the GetWord button until we either win or loose
    btnGetWord.Enabled = False
    ' Make sure the Man is not visible
    lblHead.Visible = False
    lblBody.Visible = False
    lblLegs.Visible = False
    ' Clear any messages
    lblMessage.Text = ""
    ' Clear any previous guessed letters
    lblLet1.Text = "_"
    lblLet2.Text = "_"
    lblLet3.Text = "_"
    lblLet4.Text = "_"
    lblLet5.Text = "_"
    ' Set our Global Counters to Zero
    intHangLocation = 0
    intWordLetters = 0
```

Note that the last two statements are Zeroing out the integer In Class Variables we declared at the top of the program.

The entire Method looks like:

```vb
Private Sub btnGetWord_Click(ByVal sender As System.Object, ByVal e As System.EventArgs) Handles btnGetWord.Click
    ' We declare an Array with 5 different 5 character words
    Dim strWords() As String = {"SHARP", "WORDS", "MICRO", "BRAIN", "GRAPE"}
    ' Instantiate a new random number
    Dim rNum As Random = New Random()
    ' Declare and get a Random number between 0 and 4 (<5)
    Dim intNum As Integer = rNum.Next(0, 5)
    ' Randomly choose a word to guess
    strWord2Guess = strWords(intNum)
    ' Make our Guess controls useable since we now have a word
    btnGuess.Enabled = True
    txtGuess.Enabled = True
    ' Disable the GetWord button until we either win or loose
    btnGetWord.Enabled = False
    ' Make sure the Man is not visible
    lblHead.Visible = False
    lblBody.Visible = False
    lblLegs.Visible = False
    ' Clear any messages
    lblMessage.Text = ""
    ' Clear any previous guessed letters
    lblLet1.Text = "_"
    lblLet2.Text = "_"
    lblLet3.Text = "_"
    lblLet4.Text = "_"
    lblLet5.Text = "_"
    ' Set our Global Counters to Zero
    intHangLocation = 0
    intWordLetters = 0
End Sub
```

Remember to Save! =

At this point we have the word we want to guess, the "man" is invisible, and our Guess button and textbox are ready to allow us to guess the word. So let's program the guessing – go back to the Form Designer and double-click the btnGuess button and you will be taken to the code page with this code:

```vb
Private Sub btnGuess_Click(ByVal sender As System.Object, ByVal e As System.EventArgs) Handles btnGuess.Click

End Sub
```

When we click our btnGuess button, like our previous EasyGame program, we want to check to see if someone entered a character into the textbox and if they did not, send a message back to the user to tell them they must enter a character. Type the following code;

```
Private Sub btnGuess_Click(ByVal sender As System.Object, ByVal e As …
    ' Check to see if the user put something into the Guess box
    If txtGuess.Text = "" Then
        lblMessage.Visible = True
        lblMessage.Text = "You must enter a Guess"
        lblMessage.ForeColor = Color.Red
        Return
    End If
```

As before, if `txtGuess.Text = ""` or there is nothing in the txtGuess textbox, we want to tell the user they made a mistake.

Next we want to find out if the character we entered in the txtGuess textbox is one of the letters in our word. To do this, we use a built-in function called **InStr** and this will return the position of the letter in our word. If the character we guessed is not part of the word, the InStr function returns Zero (0) as the position.

```
Dim pos As Integer = InStr(1, strWord2Guess, txtGuess.Text)
```

To break this statement down, we declare an integer variable `Dim pos As Integer` which will tell us the position of the letter we entered in the word we are guessing. We use the function InStr to see if the guess we entered is in the word and we look for the character we guessed starting at position 1 of the word,

```
InStr(1, strWord2Guess, txtGuess.Text)
```

where `strWord2Guess` is the word we are guessing, `InStr` is the function we use to inspect the word with the character we guessed, `txtGuess.Text`, **starting at position**, "(1," **of the word we are trying to guess.**

Remember I said earlier if the character we entered is not in the word being guessed, the InStr function will return a Zero (0) so the next thing we want to do is check to see if the position returned is greater than Zero (0) because if it is, the letter we entered is in the word we are trying to guess. This can be done with a very simple If statement:

```
If pos > 0 Then
Else
End If
```

where if pos is greater than 0 then we will have a correct guess and if not (Else), we will have to add a piece to the man that is being hung. Let's tackle the If True first which means we guessed right. In our Hangman game, we want to show the word that we are guessing a letter at a time but put the letter in the right position. On our Form, we created Five labels, lblLet1, lblLet2, lblLet3, lblLet4 and lblLet5, each label represents a letter in our word. If the letter we entered as a guess is in the word we are guessing, we want to assign that letter to the proper label so that the user of our game can see the word as it is being formed. As an example, if our word is "SHARP" and we guessed "A", we want to put A into lblLet3, or the third position in our word. To demonstrate, our screen will look like:

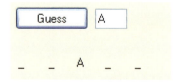

If our next guess was S, then we would see our Form look like:

Until the entire word is guessed:

To place the letter in the proper label so our word will display the way it is written, we need to use the position variable to determine the label the letter should go into. This can be done a few ways. We could use an If statement where we would test the integer pos and IF pos is 1, then put the letter into lblLet1, if pos is 2, put the letter into lblLet2, and so on. To make it easy for us to determine which character we guessed goes into what label, let's use the Select Case statement. The Select statement evaluates the variable fed to it and uses Case statements to allow you to tell the program what you want to look for and to do. A switch statement looks like:

> Select *variable*
>   case *condition*
>   do things
>   case *condition*
>   do things
> End Select

In our program, we want to test the pos variable and if pos = 1, put the guessed letter into lblLet1.

```
If pos > 0 Then
    Select pos
        Case 1
            lblLet1.Text = txtGuess.Text
            intWordLetters += 1
        Case 2
            lblLet2.Text = txtGuess.Text
            intWordLetters += 1
```

Above we are saying if pos is greater than 0, the letter we guessed is in our word; therefore, evaluate pos and if pos is 1, put that letter in the label lblLet1. If pos is 2, then put that letter in label lblLet2, and so on. However, we have one more statement under each Case:

```
intWordLetters += 1
```

Remember we declared intWordLetters at the very top of our code page under the Class declaration. We are using this variable as a counter and when we have guessed all the letters in our 5 letter word, we can declare the user a winner and we know the word has been fully guessed. We will see the code that checks if we have guessed all 5 letters later. Visual Basic allows us to increment an integer very easily. We could write something like x = x + 1 which would take whatever value is in x and add one (1) to it. "+= 1" does the same thing and is a shortcut. So rather than state x = x + 1, we can say the same thing as x += 1. Each time we find a letter, we add one (1) to intWordLetters.

We repeat this for all 5 letters:

```
If pos > 0 Then
    Select pos
        Case 1
            lblLet1.Text = txtGuess.Text
            intWordLetters += 1
        Case 2
            lblLet2.Text = txtGuess.Text
            intWordLetters += 1
        Case 3
            lblLet3.Text = txtGuess.Text
            intWordLetters += 1
        Case 4
            lblLet4.Text = txtGuess.Text
            intWordLetters += 1
        Case 5
            lblLet5.Text = txtGuess.Text
            intWordLetters += 1
    End Select
```

If pos is equal to Zero, we perform an else and this is where we start to add the man figure under the gallows. Again, we can use a switch statement.

```
Else
    intHangLocation += 1
    Select Case intHangLocation
        Case 1
```

```
            lblHead.Visible = True
            lblHead.Text = "O"
        Case 2
            lblBody.Visible = True
            lblBody.Text = "  |"
```

Like with the In Class variable intWordLetters, we declared the In Class variable intHangLocation at the top of the code page under the Class declaration. We will use the integer variable intHangLocation to keep track of where we are at with missed letters. When a letter is not in the word, the computer will execute the Else statement. intHangLocation starts as Zero (0), we set this in the `btnGetWord_Click` Method and the first time we execute the Else statement, intHangLocation will be 0 + 1 = 1; therefore, we will perform the first case statement which makes the label lblHead visible and makes sure it is an O which looks like a head of the man on the Form.

The next time we miss a letter, intHangLocation is already one (1) so we add 1 to it and it becomes two (2); therefore, case 2 is executed, and here we make the label lblBody visible and assign it a vertical line to represent a body. Notice that there are two blanks or spaces (" ") before the vertical line ("|"). This is to align the vertical line with the head above so that the "man" looks correct.

We continue on so as letters are missed, the body is formed:

```
    Else
        intHangLocation += 1
        Select Case intHangLocation
            Case 1
                lblHead.Visible = True
                lblHead.Text = "O"
            Case 2
                lblBody.Visible = True
                lblBody.Text = "  |"
            Case 3
                lblBody.Text = "/|"
            Case 4
                lblBody.Text = "/|>"
            Case 5
                lblLegs.Visible = True
                lblLegs.Text = "/"
            Case 6
```

```vbnet
            lblLegs.Text = "/>"
            lblMessage.Text = "You lost!"
            lblMessage.ForeColor = Color.Blue
            btnGuess.Enabled = False
            txtGuess.Text = ""
            txtGuess.Enabled = False
            btnGetWord.Enabled = True
    End Select
```

In the instance of the last missed chance, we can declare the user as having lost the game, and turn on and off the appropriate buttons and textbox.

After we have checked if the user has correctly guessed the letter in the word, we check to see if all letters have been guessed and if they have, declare the user a winner and like above, turn on and off the appropriate buttons and textbox so the user has the opportunity to try a new word.

```vbnet
    ' If your Word Count is 5 then you have won
    If intWordLetters = 5 Then
        lblMessage.Text = "You WON!"
        lblMessage.ForeColor = Color.Green
        btnGuess.Enabled = False
        txtGuess.Text = ""
        txtGuess.Enabled = False
        btnGetWord.Enabled = True
    End If
```

That's it, your Hangman game is now complete. The entire code for this program looks like the following:

```vbnet
Public Class Form1
    ' Add these three variables for use througout the class
    Public strWord2Guess As String
    Public intHangLocation As Integer
    Public intWordLetters As Integer

    Private Sub Form1_Load(ByVal sender As System.Object, ByVal e As System.EventArgs) Handles MyBase.Load
        lblHead.Visible = False
        lblBody.Visible = False
        lblLegs.Visible = False
        btnGuess.Enabled = False
        txtGuess.Enabled = False
    End Sub
```

```vb
    Private Sub btnGetWord_Click(ByVal sender As System.Object, ByVal e As
System.EventArgs) Handles btnGetWord.Click
        ' We declare an Array with 5 different 5 character words
        Dim strWords() As String = {"SHARP", "WORDS", "MICRO", "BRAIN", "GRAPE"}
        ' Instantiate a new random number
        Dim rNum As Random = New Random()
        ' Declare and get a Random number between 0 and 4 (<5)
        Dim intNum As Integer = rNum.Next(0, 5)
        ' Randomly choose a word to guess
        strWord2Guess = strWords(intNum)
        ' Make our Guess controls useable since we now have a word
        btnGuess.Enabled = True
        txtGuess.Enabled = True
        ' Disable the GetWord button until we either win or loose
        btnGetWord.Enabled = False
        ' Make sure the Man is not visible
        lblHead.Visible = False
        lblBody.Visible = False
        lblLegs.Visible = False
        ' Clear any messages
        lblMessage.Text = ""
        ' Clear any previsous guessed letters
        lblLet1.Text = "_"
        lblLet2.Text = "_"
        lblLet3.Text = "_"
        lblLet4.Text = "_"
        lblLet5.Text = "_"
        ' Set our Global Counters to Zero
        intHangLocation = 0
        intWordLetters = 0
    End Sub

    Private Sub btnGuess_Click(ByVal sender As System.Object, ByVal e As
System.EventArgs) Handles btnGuess.Click
        ' Check to see if the user put something into the Guess box
        If txtGuess.Text = "" Then
            lblMessage.Visible = True
            lblMessage.Text = "You must enter a Guess"
            lblMessage.ForeColor = Color.Red
            Return
        End If
        ' Find if your guess letter is in the word
        Dim pos As Integer = InStr(1, strWord2Guess, txtGuess.Text)
        ' If pos is not 0, means that the letter is in the word
        If pos > 0 Then
            Select pos
                Case 1
                    lblLet1.Text = txtGuess.Text
                    intWordLetters += 1
                Case 2
                    lblLet2.Text = txtGuess.Text
                    intWordLetters += 1
                Case 3
                    lblLet3.Text = txtGuess.Text
                    intWordLetters += 1
                Case 4
                    lblLet4.Text = txtGuess.Text
                    intWordLetters += 1
```

```vbnet
                    Case 5
                        lblLet5.Text = txtGuess.Text
                        intWordLetters += 1
                End Select
            Else ' letter is not in the word
                intHangLocation += 1
                Select Case intHangLocation
                    Case 1
                        lblHead.Visible = True
                        lblHead.Text = "O"
                    Case 2
                        lblBody.Visible = True
                        lblBody.Text = "  |"
                    Case 3
                        lblBody.Text = "/|"
                    Case 4
                        lblBody.Text = "/|>"
                    Case 5
                        lblLegs.Visible = True
                        lblLegs.Text = "/"
                    Case 6
                        lblLegs.Text = "/>"
                        lblMessage.Text = "You lost!"
                        lblMessage.ForeColor = Color.Blue
                        btnGuess.Enabled = False
                        txtGuess.Text = ""
                        txtGuess.Enabled = False
                        btnGetWord.Enabled = True
                End Select
            End If
            ' If your Word Count is 5 then you have won
            If intWordLetters = 5 Then
                lblMessage.Text = "You WON!"
                lblMessage.ForeColor = Color.Green
                btnGuess.Enabled = False
                txtGuess.Text = ""
                txtGuess.Enabled = False
                btnGetWord.Enabled = True
            End If
    End Sub
End Class
```

Remember to Save! =

Now let's play! Start your program,

Press F5   or    or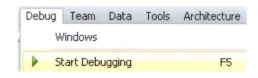

74

Press the button "Get Word".

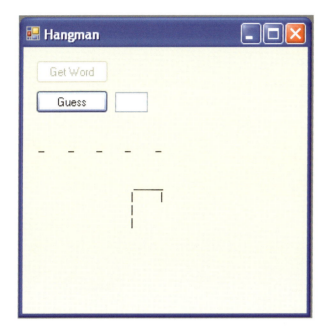

Enter a letter in the Textbox and click the button labeled Guess. Make sure you enter your letters as capital letters. In this case, Visual Basic is case sensitive and "A" is not the same as "a". If you filled your array with words that were all capitalized or all lower case, enter your letters the same in the textbox.

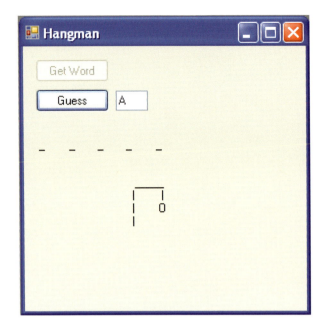

I entered "A" in the textbox and "A" was not found in my word so the head of the man is displayed.

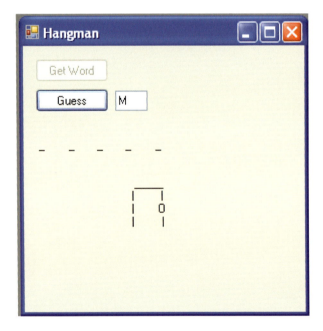

I entered "M" in the textbox and "M" was not found in my word so the body of the man is displayed.

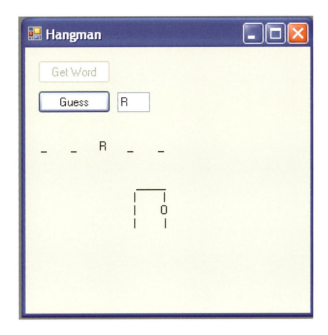

I enter "R" and "R" is part of the word I am guessing so it shows up as part of the word.

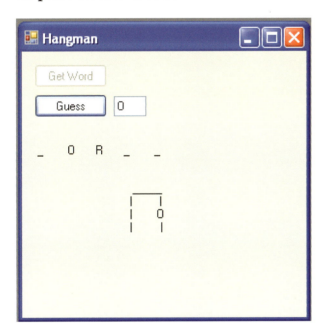

I guess "O" and it is also part of the word.

Now I think I know what it is?

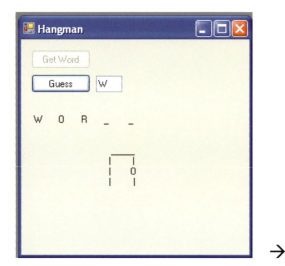 →

And …

We won! We are ready to get a new word and try again! Click "Get Word" and you can start a new game of Hangman.

Remember to Save! =

> More Fun!
>
> **Here are some suggestions to enhance your program. Try these and figure out how to program:**
>
> - How would you guess 6 letter words? 7 letter words?
>
> - How could you check the length of the word and then guess for that size? In other words, you may choose a 5 letter word the first time and a 7 letter word the next time.

Chapter 3 Definition Review

Enable Property
Setting a control property as control.**Enable** = true will allow the control to be used on the form. If the control.Enabled= false, the control will still display on the form but will not be accessible.

Array
An **Array** is used to store a number of items of the same data type. Arrays always start with an index of Zero (0).

In Class Variable
An **In Class** variable is a way to declare and use a variable to store a value that is accessible by all Methods within the Class.

InStr
InStr is a built-in system function that determines the position of a letter within a string.

Select … Case
A **Select … Case** statement is used to determine a series of conditions. The syntax is

```
Select variable
  case condition
    do things
  case condition
    do things
End Select
```

4. Tic Tac Toe

To reinforce the skills that you have learned and to learn how to perform complete program development, we are going to create the classic Tic Tac Toe game. I'm sure you know how to play this game but let's discuss the strategy and how the game is played. Programming should always start with **Learning** how the game works and creating a **Design** that tells the programmer what the user wishes the program to do. If someone came to you and said create the Ha He Hi game for me to play, you would say, "I don't know anything about that game" and you would have to find out what the pieces are that you play with, what the board looks like, what the rules were for the game - everything you need in order to create the program.

We will do this with Tic Tac Toe. Even though we know the game very well, we will learn the steps of program development using Tic Tac Toe. I think one of the early development cycles I learned was characterized as the Six (6) Its:

Step 1: Learn *It*

Step 2: Design *It*

Step 3: Code *It*

Step 4: Test and Tune *It*

Step 5: Document *It*

Step 6: Implement *It*

Using this development style, which is called the Waterfall model, we can see the first two steps should be done before programming even begins; step 3 is coding the program, the other 5 steps all must be done to create a program that can be put out there for others to use. Let's use these steps to create a Tic Tac Toe program.

Step 1: Learn It

Ourselves, a person, or a Company that has hired us, is asking us to program Tic Tac Toe so the first thing we need to do is Learn how Tic Tac Toe works. One of the most common mistakes every programmer can make is they think they know how something works already but it is always valuable to listen to the person who is asking you to program and learn from them how they think something works. For the purposes of this exercise, I will play the role of the person asking to program Tic Tac Toe. I describe Tic Tac Toe as follows:

"Tic Tac Toe is a game that has 9 squares arranged so that there are 3 squares on the top, sides and bottom with one square in the middle like this picture:

The game has two players, one represents the Xs and the second player represents Os. The first player starts and places an X into any square and then the second places an O into any square that does not already have an X in it. The first player places another X into an unused square, the second player then places an O into any unused square. Alternating placing Xs and Os into unused squares continues until one player gets three of their letters into a line, or three in a row. Rows can be horizontal, diagonal or vertical. Here are examples of wins:

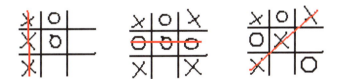

If neither player gets three in a row, the game is considered a draw and no one wins or loses – a tie."

With the description above, we now have an understanding from the person asking us to program how they think the game is played.

Step 2: Design It

From the person asking us to program, we now have a description of what they want us to program. The next step in software development is the Design. The Design is how the programmer interprets what the person asking them to program wants done; in other words, "Step 1: Learn It" is a description from the person asking for the program and "Step 2: Design It" is a description of what is going to happen from the programmer.

Let's create the Design. In the Design, we actually describe the programming in computer terms but without actually programming. How do we do that? Let's start with the boxes that make up the 9 squares where we place an X or an O. How can we do this? There are probably many ways but we already know how to use a Button and how clicking a button allows us to put code behind it. So we can say something like the following:

We will create a Form

On the form we will place Nine buttons arranged so there are three buttons on top, three in the middle and three at the bottom so it will look like:

We will size the buttons so they are square and change the Font size so the letter that appears inside fills the button square.

A button will look like when a letter is displayed.

When the user clicks on a button, the program will check to see if there is something there already and if it is, we will ignore that click. If there is nothing already in that square, we will put either an X or an O depending on if it's Xs or Os turn.

We will always start with X and keep track if it is Xs or Os turn with an in class variable. If this variable is equal to Zero, it is Xs turn, if it is One, it is Os turn. Every time we assign an X or an O to a square (button), we will change the variable to be Zero or One depending on which letter we assign to that square (button).

Each time a square is assigned an X or an O, we will use a Function that we will create that looks to see if there are any Xs or Os that are three is a row. To accomplish this search, we will arrange and name the squares (buttons) as such:

1	2	3
4	5	6
7	8	9

We will need to look at eight directions to see if there are three in a row:

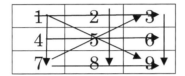

- if button1 = button2 = button3 where each button can be all X or all O
- if button1 = button4 = button7
- if button2 = button5 = button8
- if button3 = button6 = button9
- if button4 = button5 = button6
- if button7 = button8 = button9
- if button7 = button5 = button3

If any of these conditions are true, then player X is the winner if the last button clicked was from player X, or player O is the winner if the last button clicked is from player O.

To determine if this game is concluded in a draw, we must keep track of the number of squares marked. If there are 9 squares marked, and no three in a row, we can declare the game a draw.

In addition we will create a method for disabling the squares when there is a winner and that tells the user they have won, as well as, a Clear button to start a game over or to start a new game.

This should be a fairly well thought out description of what we are going to do from a programming point of view. We have tried to look at every aspect of what we want our program to do and how to do it. If you were hired by someone to create this program, typically you would sit down with that person and go over what you have written. Because it is in simple words, and the hiring person would not be looking at code, everyone should be able to understand what you are doing and why. Once both parties agree that what you are programming is exactly what they want, then you can begin to create the program using your description.

Step 3: Code It
The Form

First, like our other two programs, we want to start Visual Studio and create a project. Click New Project:

Make sure your project type is Visual Basic > Windows, select the Windows Forms Application template and name your project *TicTacToe*, then click OK.

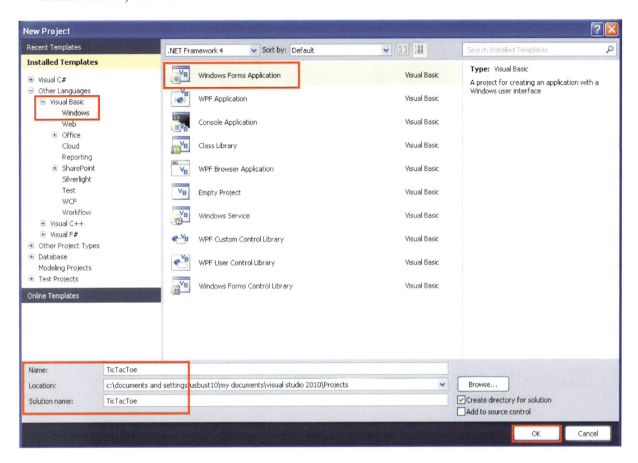

You should see something familiar like:

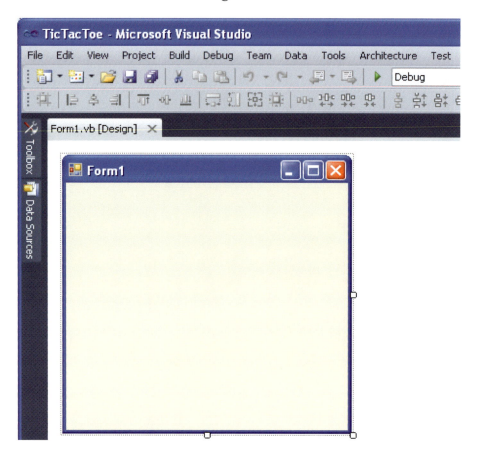

Click on the Form and let's change the Text for the form to "Tic Tac Toe".

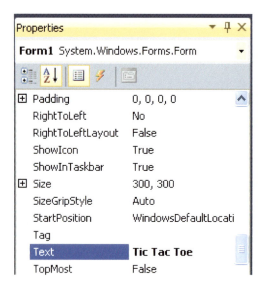

As we said in our Design, we will place Nine (9) buttons on the form, three on top, three in the middle and three on the bottom. The easiest way to do this is to create the first button so that you can copy and paste it to create the other eight. Let's drag a button to the form.

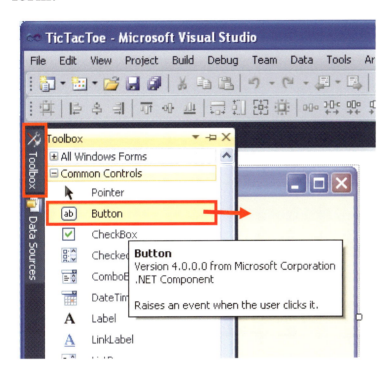

And place in the upper left.

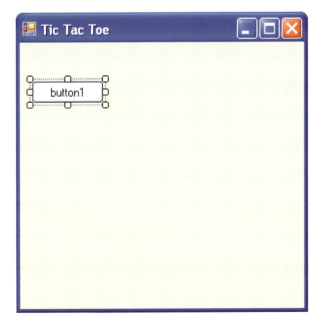

We want to resize the button so it looks square. Do this by moving the cursor over the lower little square at the bottom center of the button control, clicking and you will see an arrow. Drag the button down so it forms a square.

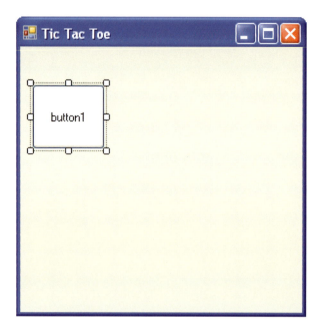

Now let's go to the Properties and change the Font size to 24. You can change the Text to X to see what it looks like.

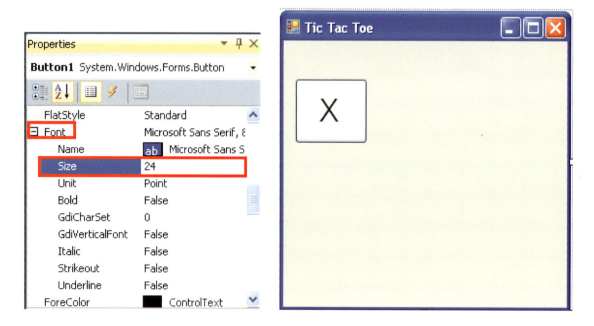

Change the Text so nothing appears.

Now right click on the button (be careful not to double-click) and choose Copy.

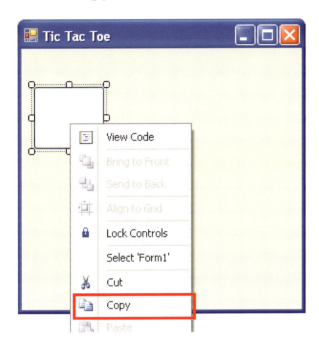

Then right click on the Form and choose Paste

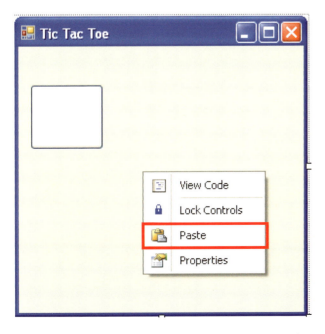

The results will look like:

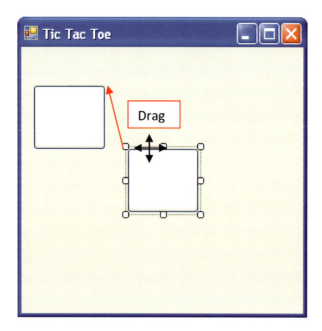

Put the cursor over the top line of the button (button2) that you just pasted until you see something like ✥

Then click your mouse and drag into position alongside the first button.

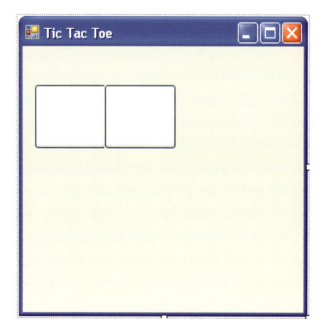

Copy and Paste again to create button3, then Drag next to button2.

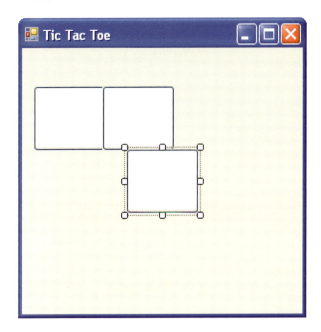

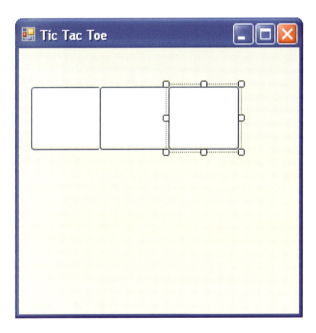

Copy and Paste the forth button so you end up like:

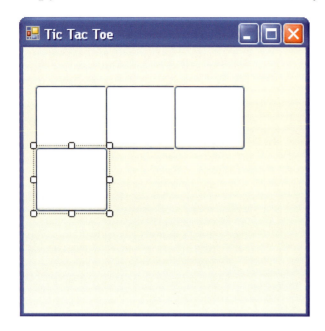

Do this 5 more times until you have the following:

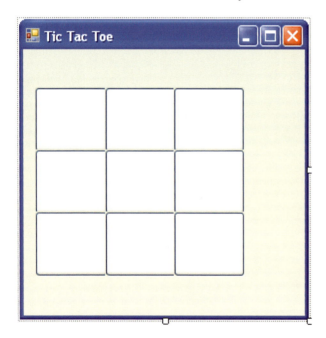

This should be in the order so that the following naming is true:

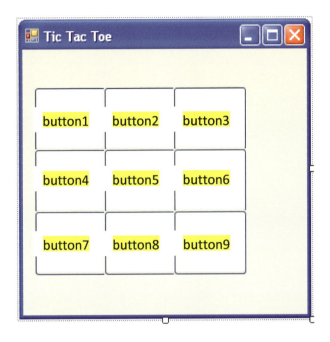

It is very important to have the names in this order so when we look for three-in-a-row, we can use the button names to check the contents of each. This follows our Design when we said we would check for three-in-a-row by looking at button1=button2=button3, button1=button4=button7, and so on.

Next we will add another button that will be used to reset the game.

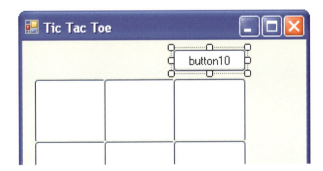

Let's name this button btnClear and change the Text to "Clear".

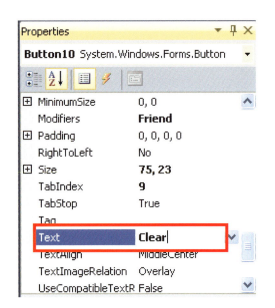 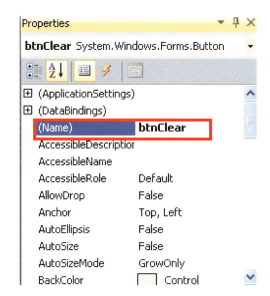

And on the Form, it looks like:

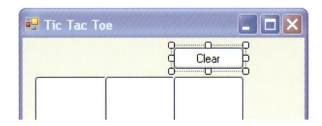

At the bottom, let's add a label called lblMessage:

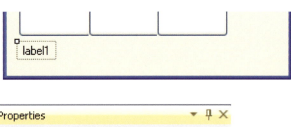

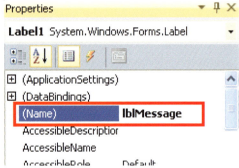

And we will put "Message" as the text.

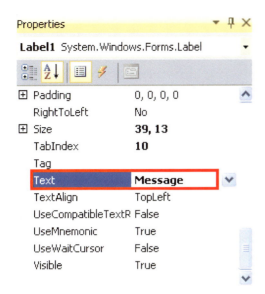

Our form is complete and looks like:

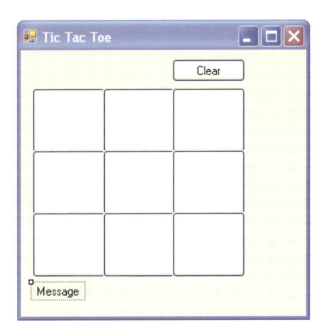

The Code Behind

Double-click the Form (on the form where there are no controls) and we will get the Form1_Load method as we have seen before.

```vb
Private Sub Form1_Load(ByVal sender As System.Object, ByVal e As System.EventArgs) Handles MyBase.Load

End Sub
```

As before, we want to add code that will get us started as the program starts. Enter the following code:

```vb
Private Sub Form1_Load(ByVal sender As System.Object, ByVal e As System.EventArgs) …
    ' We will use the XO veriable to determine if we are X or O
    ' XO = 0 = X, XO = 1 = O
    intXO = 0
    ' We will use the DrawGame variable as a counter and when we
    ' reach 9, we know there are no more squares to click.
    intDrawGame = 0
    lblMessage.Text = "X is up"
End Sub
```

Wait, we haven't declared a variable labeled intXO or intDrawGame? You can see this because they will have red squiggly lines under them. Let's create global In Class variables. Just below Class Form1, declare these variables as Integer types:

```vb
Public Class Form1
    Public intXO As Integer
    Public intDrawGame As Integer

    Private Sub Form1_Load(ByVal sender As System.Object, ByVal e As System.EventArgs) Handles MyBase.Load
        ' We will use the XO veriable to determine if we are X or O
        ' XO = 0 = X, XO = 1 = O
        intXO = 0
        ' We will use the DrawGame variable as a counter and when we
        ' reach 9, we know there are no more squares to click.
        intDrawGame = 0
        lblMessage.Text = "X is up"
    End Sub
End Class
```

Now the red squiggly lines will be gone because these variables are declared and global to the Class. We can use these variables to tell us when whether it is Xs or Os turn, and when we have a game that ends in a tie or draw. Last, in the code above, we let the users know that X is up first.

We want to program the buttons next. Go back to the Form and double-click button1.

```vb
Private Sub Button1_Click(ByVal sender As System.Object, ByVal e As System.EventArgs) Handles Button1.Click

End Sub
```

First we want to check to see if this square (button) has been clicked already so we add an If statement that checks and if this button has been clicked before, we simply ignore the click:

```vb
Private Sub Button1_Click(ByVal sender As System.Object, ByVal e As System.EventArgs)
    ' Check to see if button has been clicked already
    If Button1.Text = "X" Or Button1.Text = "O" Then Return
End Sub
```

Looking at the If statement above it says, if button1 is an X or an O then return which just gives back control of the program to the user. Nothing else changes and it's still the same person's turn.

Next, after we know the button is not X or O, we want to check to see who's turn it is and then mark the square (button) accordingly. Remember we created a global Class variable named intXO and we decided that if it is Zero (0), it is Xs turn and if it is One (1), it is Os turn. In our Form_load, we set intXO = 0 so to start, it is Xs turn. So if intXO = 0 then we want to put an X in the square or the text of the button. If intXO is 1 then we want to put O in the square or the text of the button.

We add another If ... Else statement to see if intXO is Zero (0) or One (1) so we know how to mark the square (button):

```vb
Private Sub Button1_Click(ByVal sender As System.Object, ByVal e As …
    ' Check to see if button has been clicked already
    If Button1.Text = "X" Or Button1.Text = "O" Then Return
    ' If XO = 0 then it is Xs turn, if not it is Os turn
    If intXO = 0 Then
        Button1.Text = "X"
        intXO = 1
        lblMessage.Text = "O is up!"
    Else
        Button1.Text = "O"
        intXO = 0
        lblMessage.Text = "X is up!"
    End If
End Sub
```

Looking at the code in the box above, we can see the first check is if intXO = 0 and if it is, we change the button text to X, change intXO to One (it is now Os turn) and tell the user that O is up to play next. The Else statement does the opposite – if intXO is not Zero, it must be One so currently it is Os turn and we change the button text to O, change intXO to Zero to tell the program it is Xs turn now and let the user know that X is up next.

We could take this code and copy/paste it for each button, which we will do later, but before we do that, we need to do additional steps each time we click a button. One of the things we need to check is if this square created a winning situation of three in a row. Since we have to check for three in a row each and every time a button is clicked, we are better off to create a function that allows us to call it, have it check for a three in a row match and if true, there is a match, we declare the user a winner, if not we continue on. A Function is a Method that is declared as a data type (string, integer, boolean, …) that we can call and it returns a value that we can use to determine a condition in our program. A lot to say there but it is simpler than it is to explain. Let's digress for a moment and create a function we can use to determine if we have three in a row. We will call our Method "CheckForWinner". In Visual Basic we do this by declaring the

Method much the same way we see our Methods for Form_Load and Button_Clicks are declared but as a Function and as a variable data type:

```
Function CheckForWinner(parameters) As Boolean
```

Our Function is being declared Boolean, or the result from calling this Function is going to be either True or False. So when we call CheckForWinner, we will expect to be told that it is True and we have three in a row thus we have a winner, or False, we do not have three in a row and the last player is not a winner, or there is not a winner yet.

To check for three in a row, we must tell our Function CheckForWinner what Xs, Os or nothing is in our squares (buttons). To do this will we pass the Text of each square to the Function. Text is string so we will tell the Funtion we are passing it these 9 strings.

```
Function CheckForWinner(ByVal b1 As String, ByVal b2 As String, ByVal b3 As String,
ByVal b4 As String, ByVal b5 As String, ByVal b6 As String, ByVal b7 As String, ByVal b8
As String, ByVal b9 As String) As Boolean
```

b1 is the text from button1, b2 will be the text from button2, and so on until b9 is the text from button9. We will pass the text from each button, 1 through 9.

We can then check our buttons and see if we have any matches. As in our Design It, we have already defined what buttons we need to check and in what order. The first is if button1 is equal to button 2 and button2 is equal to button3, we know we have a winner or three in a row and can return true to the calling method.

←1	2	→3
4	5	6
7	8	9

```
If b1 = b2 And b2 = b3 Then
    Return True
End If
```

But wait, if there are no Xs or Os in these three buttons, they will be blank and equal, but if there are no Xs or Os, all this means is we have not clicked on those squares (buttons) and we do not want to declare a winner so we do one more check whereas if button1, button2, and button3 are equal, we check to make sure they are not all three blank and if they are not all three blank, we then can declare the user the winner:

```
If b1 = b2 And b2 = b3 Then
    If b1 <> "" And b2 <> "" And b3 <> "" Then Return True
End If
```

Let's dissect his a little deeper. The first line is checking to see if button1 is the same as button2 and then we check to see if button2 is the same as button3. If these were all Xs or all Os, we would have three in a row and a winner. However, we need to check to make sure each of these buttons is not " " or blank because if all three are blank, we just have not played those buttons yet. In programs, a blank is a value and we must check for blank as a value at times.

To say it again, if all three buttons are the same and all three buttons are not blank, we have three in a row and can return true.

Conditional Operators:
Operators allow us to combine conditions. In our programs we are using the following:

Logical Operators
    And, example   *if x = 0 AND y = 0 Then*, both conditions must be true
    Or, example   *if x = 0 OR y = 0 Then*, only one condition must be true

Relational Operators
    Equals is =, example *if x = 0 Then*, x must be zero to be true
    Not Equal is <>, example *if x <> 0 Then*, x can be anything but 0 to be true

We need to do the same for all possible combinations. The next set of buttons we look at is to check of button1, button4 and button7 are the same.

	1	2	3
	4	5	6
	7	8	9

```vb
    If b1 = b4 And b4 = b7 Then
        If b1 <> "" And b4 <> "" And b7 <> "" Then Return True
    End If
```

Again, like last time, we want to make sure that these buttons are not all blank before we decide there is a winner and return true. Here is the entire code with all the combinations:

```vb
' We check for three is a row to see if we have a winner
    Function CheckForWinner(ByVal b1 As String, ByVal b2 As String, ByVal b3 As String, ByVal b4 As String, ByVal b5 As String, ByVal b6 As String, ByVal b7 As String, ByVal b8 As String, ByVal b9 As String) As Boolean
        If b1 = b2 And b2 = b3 Then
            If b1 <> "" And b2 <> "" And b3 <> "" Then Return True
        End If
        If b1 = b4 And b4 = b7 Then
            If b1 <> "" And b4 <> "" And b7 <> "" Then Return True
        End If
        If b1 = b5 And b5 = b9 Then
            If b1 <> "" And b5 <> "" And b9 <> "" Then Return True
        End If
        If b2 = b5 And b5 = b8 Then
            If b2 <> "" And b5 <> "" And b8 <> "" Then Return True
        End If
        If b3 = b6 And b6 = b9 Then
            If b3 <> "" And b6 <> "" And b9 <> "" Then Return True
        End If
        If b4 = b5 And b5 = b6 Then
            If b4 <> "" And b5 <> "" And b6 <> "" Then Return True
        End If
        If b7 = b5 And b5 = b3 Then
            If b7 <> "" And b5 <> "" And b3 <> "" Then Return True
        End If
        If b7 = b8 And b8 = b9 Then
            If b7 <> "" And b8 <> "" And b9 <> "" Then Return True
        End If
        Return False
    End Function
```

If we check all the combinations and none are true, and we have not returned to the calling Method with a True, then we return False (`Return False`) to tell the calling method that we do not have a winner.

You can place this Function code anywhere in your program as long as it is outside of any other method. I put mine right after the Form1_Load method.

```vb
    Private Sub Form1_Load(ByVal sender As System.Object, ByVal e As System.EventArgs) Handles MyBase.Load
        ' We will use the XO veriable to determine if we are X or O
        ' XO = 0 = X, XO = 1 = O
        intXO = 0
        ' We will use the DrawGame variable as a counter and when we
        ' reach 9, we know there are no more squares to click.
        intDrawGame = 0
        lblMessage.Text = "X is up"
    End Sub

    ' We check for three is a row to see if we have a winner
    Function CheckForWinner(ByVal b1 As String, ByVal b2 As String, ByVal b3 As String, ByVal b4 As String, ByVal b5 As String, ByVal b6 As String, ByVal b7 As String, ByVal b8 As String, ByVal b9 As String) As Boolean
        If b1 = b2 And b2 = b3 Then
            If b1 <> "" And b2 <> "" And b3 <> "" Then Return True
        End If
```

Let's jump back to our button1_click method. We can put in code to check if we have three in a row now.

```vb
        ' Is there three in a row?
        Dim ThreeinaRow As Boolean = CheckForWinner(Button1.Text, Button2.Text, Button3.Text, Button4.Text, Button5.Text, Button6.Text, Button7.Text, Button8.Text, Button9.Text)
```

We declare a variable as boolean (true or false) named ThreeinaRow and use our function CheckForWinner to assign ThreeinaRow either true or false. We pass the contents of the Text property from each of our Buttons to the CheckForWinner function so we can find if any combination of three is X or O. If ThreeinaRow is true, we have a winner, if not, we bypass and continue the game. To check if we have a winner, we use an If statement where if we are X, we let the player using Xs know they have won Else we let the player using Os know they have won:

```
    If ThreeinaRow = True Then
        If intXO = 1 Then
            lblMessage.Text = "X Wins!"
        Else
            lblMessage.Text = "O Wins!"
        End If
        lblMessage.ForeColor = Color.Green
        GameOver()
        Return
    End If
```

Wait, there are some other statements after the If Then Else statement:

```
        lblMessage.ForeColor = Color.Green
        GameOver()
        Return
```

The first statement you have seen already, all we are doing is changing the label lblMessage to be green to make it more obvious we have a winner. What is GameOver? Like our functional method CheckForWinner, if we have a winner, we want to stop the game so let's create a new Method and call it GameOver.

```
Public Sub GameOver()
    Button1.Enabled = False
    Button2.Enabled = False
    Button3.Enabled = False
    Button4.Enabled = False
    Button5.Enabled = False
    Button6.Enabled = False
    Button7.Enabled = False
    Button8.Enabled = False
    Button9.Enabled = False
End Sub
```

All we want to do is to show the players that the game is over because we have a winner and to do this is to disable all the squares (buttons). GameOver can be placed anywhere in your Class, I put mine just below the CheckForWinner Method. We would repeat this code in each button_click Method so if we create a separate GameOver Method, all we need to do is to create the code once, and then call the Method every time we want to use it. In our case, we will call it in the code within each button.

The next statement is a `Return` so the program will stop and not go any further since we have a winner.

Last in our button code, we want to use the other global In Class variable we created named intDrawGame and increment it by One. If intDrawGame becomes Nine (9), then we know we have clicked on every button and since we do not have a winner, the game is a draw or a tie. Therefore we increment intDrawGame by one and then use an If statement to check if the last One we added makes it Nine (9) and if it is Nine, we can stop the game the tell the players no one won.

```vb
' Let's check to see of the game is a draw
' If intDrawGame is 9, it means that all 9 squares have been marked
intDrawGame += 1
If intDrawGame = 9 Then
    lblMessage.Text = "Game is a draw - Tie!"
    GameOver()
End If
```

Note that we used our Method GameOver again because if all Nine squares are marked, and there is no winner, the game is over.

Let's look at our entire code now for button1:

```vb
Private Sub Button1_Click(ByVal sender As System.Object, ByVal e As System.EventArgs) Handles Button1.Click
    ' Check to see if button has been clicked already
    If Button1.Text = "X" Or Button1.Text = "O" Then Return
    ' If XO = 0 then it is Xs turn, if not it is Os turn
    If intXO = 0 Then
        Button1.Text = "X"
        intXO = 1
        lblMessage.Text = "O is up!"
    Else
        Button1.Text = "O"
        intXO = 0
        lblMessage.Text = "X is up!"
    End If
    ' Is there three in a row?
    Dim ThreeinaRow As Boolean = CheckForWinner(Button1.Text, Button2.Text, Button3.Text, Button4.Text, Button5.Text, Button6.Text, Button7.Text, Button8.Text, Button9.Text)
    If ThreeinaRow = True Then
        If intXO = 1 Then
            lblMessage.Text = "X Wins!"
        Else
            lblMessage.Text = "O Wins!"
        End If
```

```vb
            lblMessage.ForeColor = Color.Green
            GameOver()
            Return
        End If
        ' Let's check to see of the game is a draw
        ' If intDrawGame is 9, it means that all 9 squares have been marked
        intDrawGame += 1
        If intDrawGame = 9 Then
            lblMessage.Text = "Game is a draw - Tie!"
            GameOver()
        End If
    End Sub
```

Go back to the Form and double-click button 2.

```vb
    Private Sub Button2_Click(ByVal sender As System.Object, ByVal e As System.EventArgs) Handles Button2.Click

    End Sub
```

Button2 is the same as button1 as far as the logic so rather than type out the same code for button2, let's just copy and past. Go back up to button1 and put the cursor on the first line after your button1_click line:

Cursor →
```vb
Private Sub Button1_Click(ByVal sender As System.Object, ByVal e As System.EventArgs)
    ' Check to see if button has been clicked already
    If Button1.Text = "X" Or Button1.Text = "O" Then Return
    ' If XO = 0 then it is Xs turn, if not it is Os turn
    If intXO = 0 Then
        Button1.Text = "X"
        intXO = 1
        lblMessage.Text = "O is up!"
```

Hold your left mouse button down and drag down to the end of your button1_click Method:

```vb
Private Sub Button1_Click(ByVal sender As System.Object, ByVal e As System.EventArgs) Handles Button1.Click
    ' Check to see if button has been clicked already
    If Button1.Text = "X" Or Button1.Text = "O" Then Return
    ' If XO = 0 then it is Xs turn, if not it is Os turn
    If intXO = 0 Then
        Button1.Text = "X"
        intXO = 1
        lblMessage.Text = "O is up!"
    Else
        Button1.Text = "O"
        intXO = 0
        lblMessage.Text = "X is up!"
    End If
    ' Is there three in a row?
    Dim ThreeinaRow As Boolean = CheckForWinner(Button1.Text, Button2.Text, Button3.Text, Button4.Text, But
    If ThreeinaRow = True Then
        If intXO = 1 Then
            lblMessage.Text = "X Wins!"
        Else
            lblMessage.Text = "O Wins!"
        End If
        lblMessage.ForeColor = Color.Green
        GameOver()
```

. . .

```vb
            lblMessage.Text = "O Wins!"
        End If
        lblMessage.ForeColor = Color.Green
        GameOver()
        Return
    End If
    ' Let's check to see of the game is a draw
    ' If DrawGame is 9, it means that all 9 squares have been marked
    intDrawGame += 1
    If intDrawGame = 9 Then
        lblMessage.Text = "Game is a draw - Tie!"
        GameOver()
    End If
End Sub
```

Once this code is highlighted as illustrated above, go to the menu at the top of your workbench and click Edit and then click Copy.

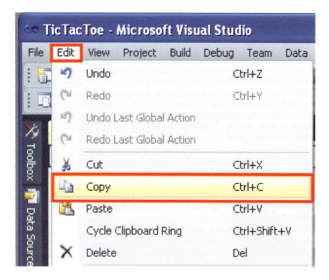

Now place your cursor after the first bracket in your button2_click code and go to the menu at the top, click Edit and then Paste.

```
Private Sub Button2_Click(ByVal sender As System.Object, ByVal e As System.EventArgs) Handles Button2.Click
    |
End Sub
```
Cursor →

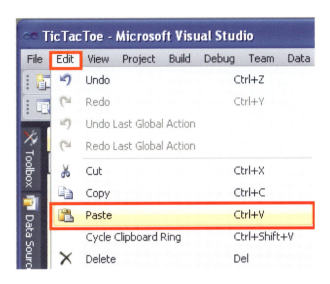

And the code from button1 is now in button2:

```vb
Private Sub Button2_Click(ByVal sender As System.Object, ByVal e As System.EventArgs) Handles Button2.Click
        ' Check to see if button has been clicked already
        If Button1.Text = "X" Or Button1.Text = "O" Then Return
        ' If XO = 0 then it is Xs turn, if not it is Os turn
        If intXO = 0 Then
            Button1.Text = "X"
            intXO = 1
            lblMessage.Text = "O is up!"
        Else
            Button1.Text = "O"
            intXO = 0
            lblMessage.Text = "X is up!"
        End If
        ' Is there three in a row?
        Dim ThreeinaRow As Boolean = CheckForWinner(Button1.Text, Button2.Text, Button3.Text, Button4.Text, Button5.Text, Button6.Text, Button7.Text, Button8.Text, Button9.Text)
        If ThreeinaRow = True Then
            If intXO = 1 Then
                lblMessage.Text = "X Wins!"
            Else
                lblMessage.Text = "O Wins!"
            End If
            lblMessage.ForeColor = Color.Green
            GameOver()
            Return
```

```vb
        End If
        ' Let's check to see of the game is a draw
        ' If intDrawGame is 9, it means that all 9 squares have been marked
        intDrawGame += 1
        If intDrawGame = 9 Then
            lblMessage.Text = "Game is a draw - Tie!"
            GameOver()
        End If
    End Sub
```

However we need to change the code in button2 that refers to button1 to button2 like the first line: `If button1.Text = "X" OR button1.Text = "O"`

Change this to   `If button2.Text = "X" OR button2.Text = "O"`

Go through the code in button2 and every where you see button1, make it button2, except where you are calling CheckForWinner – leave these button references as they are. You will have the following code and I have highlighted where you would change the numbers (4 locations) as `button2.Text`:

```vb
    Private Sub Button2_Click(ByVal sender As System.Object, ByVal e As System.EventArgs) Handles Button2.Click
        ' Check to see if button has been clicked already
        If Button2.Text = "X" Or Button2.Text = "O" Then Return
        ' If XO = 0 then it is Xs turn, if not it is Os turn
        If intXO = 0 Then
            Button2.Text = "X"
            intXO = 1
            lblMessage.Text = "O is up!"
        Else
            Button2.Text = "O"
            intXO = 0
            lblMessage.Text = "X is up!"
        End If
        ' Is there three in a row?
        Dim ThreeinaRow As Boolean = CheckForWinner(Button1.Text, Button2.Text, Button3.Text, Button4.Text, Button5.Text, Button6.Text, Button7.Text, Button8.Text, Button9.Text)
        If ThreeinaRow = True Then
            If intXO = 1 Then
                lblMessage.Text = "X Wins!"
            Else
                lblMessage.Text = "O Wins!"
            End If
            lblMessage.ForeColor = Color.Green
            GameOver()
            Return
        End If
        ' Let's check to see of the game is a draw
        ' If intDrawGame is 9, it means that all 9 squares have been marked
        intDrawGame += 1
```

```vb
        If intDrawGame = 9 Then
            lblMessage.Text = "Game is a draw - Tie!"
            GameOver()
        End If
    End Sub
```

Repeat this process for each button. Go to the form, double-click on the button (example button3), copy the code from the previous button, paste the code in the button code you just created, and change the Four places where the button number should match the button you are coding. Button5_click would be:

```vb
    Private Sub Button5_Click(ByVal sender As System.Object, ByVal e As System.EventArgs) Handles Button5.Click
        ' Check to see if button has been clicked already
        If Button5.Text = "X" Or Button5.Text = "O" Then Return
        ' If XO = 0 then it is Xs turn, if not it is Os turn
        If intXO = 0 Then
            Button5.Text = "X"
            intXO = 1
            lblMessage.Text = "O is up!"
        Else
            Button5.Text = "O"
            intXO = 0
            lblMessage.Text = "X is up!"
        End If
        ' Is there three in a row?
        Dim ThreeinaRow As Boolean = CheckForWinner(Button1.Text, Button2.Text, Button3.Text, Button4.Text, Button5.Text, Button6.Text, Button7.Text, Button8.Text, Button9.Text)
        If ThreeinaRow = True Then
            If intXO = 1 Then
                lblMessage.Text = "X Wins!"
            Else
                lblMessage.Text = "O Wins!"
            End If
            lblMessage.ForeColor = Color.Green
            GameOver()
            Return
        End If
        ' Let's check to see of the game is a draw
        ' If intDrawGame is 9, it means that all 9 squares have been marked
        intDrawGame += 1
        If intDrawGame = 9 Then
            lblMessage.Text = "Game is a draw - Tie!"
            GameOver()
        End If
    End Sub
```

Make sure you repeat this for each button – all Nine.

Finally, we have a Clear button on our Form we need to program. Go to your Form design and double-click the Clear button.

```vb
Private Sub btnClear_Click(ByVal sender As System.Object, ByVal e As System.EventArgs) Handles btnClear.Click

End Sub
```

We will use the Clear button to reset the game. You could call this button Reset as easy as you can call it Clear. The first thing we want to do is to clear all the Os and Xs in our buttons and make the buttons enabled:

```vb
Private Sub btnClear_Click(ByVal sender As System.Object, ByVal e As System.EventArgs) Handles btnClear.Click
    ' Clear and enable the buttons
    Button1.Enabled = True
    Button2.Enabled = True
    Button3.Enabled = True
    Button4.Enabled = True
    Button5.Enabled = True
    Button6.Enabled = True
    Button7.Enabled = True
    Button8.Enabled = True
    Button9.Enabled = True
    Button1.Text = ""
    Button2.Text = ""
    Button3.Text = ""
    Button4.Text = ""
    Button5.Text = ""
    Button6.Text = ""
    Button7.Text = ""
    Button8.Text = ""
    Button9.Text = ""
```

Then we want to reset our global Class variables and tell the player using Xs the game is ready for them to start:

```vb
    ' Reset our global Class variables to Zero
    intXO = 0
    intDrawGame = 0
    ' Let X know they are first to play
    lblMessage.Text = "X is up"
    lblMessage.ForeColor = Color.Black
```

Our entire btnClear_click will be:

```vb
    Private Sub btnClear_Click(ByVal sender As System.Object, ByVal e As System.EventArgs) Handles btnClear.Click
        ' Clear and enable the buttons
        Button1.Enabled = True
        Button2.Enabled = True
        Button3.Enabled = True
        Button4.Enabled = True
        Button5.Enabled = True
        Button6.Enabled = True
        Button7.Enabled = True
        Button8.Enabled = True
        Button9.Enabled = True
        Button1.Text = ""
        Button2.Text = ""
        Button3.Text = ""
        Button4.Text = ""
        Button5.Text = ""
        Button6.Text = ""
        Button7.Text = ""
        Button8.Text = ""
        Button9.Text = ""
        ' Reset our global Class variables to Zero
        intXO = 0
        intDrawGame = 0
        ' Let X know they are first to play
        lblMessage.Text = "X is up"
        lblMessage.ForeColor = Color.Black
    End Sub
```

Now our program is complete! The whole program is:

```vb
Public Class Form1
    Public intXO As Integer
    Public intDrawGame As Integer

    Private Sub Form1_Load(ByVal sender As System.Object, ByVal e As System.EventArgs) Handles MyBase.Load
        ' We will use the XO veriable to determine if we are X or O
        ' XO = 0 = X, XO = 1 = O
        intXO = 0
        ' We will use the DrawGame variable as a counter and when we
        ' reach 9, we know there are no more squares to click.
        intDrawGame = 0
        lblMessage.Text = "X is up"
    End Sub

    ' We check for three is a row to see if we have a winner
    Function CheckForWinner(ByVal b1 As String, ByVal b2 As String, ByVal b3 As String, ByVal b4 As String, ByVal b5 As String, ByVal b6 As String, ByVal b7 As String, ByVal b8 As String, ByVal b9 As String) As Boolean
        If b1 = b2 And b2 = b3 Then
            If b1 <> "" And b2 <> "" And b3 <> "" Then Return True
        End If
```

```vb
            If b1 = b4 And b4 = b7 Then
                If b1 <> "" And b4 <> "" And b7 <> "" Then Return True
            End If
            If b1 = b5 And b5 = b9 Then
                If b1 <> "" And b5 <> "" And b9 <> "" Then Return True
            End If
            If b2 = b5 And b5 = b8 Then
                If b2 <> "" And b5 <> "" And b8 <> "" Then Return True
            End If
            If b3 = b6 And b6 = b9 Then
                If b3 <> "" And b6 <> "" And b9 <> "" Then Return True
            End If
            If b4 = b5 And b5 = b6 Then
                If b4 <> "" And b5 <> "" And b6 <> "" Then Return True
            End If
            If b7 = b5 And b5 = b3 Then
                If b7 <> "" And b5 <> "" And b3 <> "" Then Return True
            End If
            If b7 = b8 And b8 = b9 Then
                If b7 <> "" And b8 <> "" And b9 <> "" Then Return True
            End If
            Return False
        End Function

    Public Sub GameOver()
        Button1.Enabled = False
        Button2.Enabled = False
        Button3.Enabled = False
        Button4.Enabled = False
        Button5.Enabled = False
        Button6.Enabled = False
        Button7.Enabled = False
        Button8.Enabled = False
        Button9.Enabled = False
    End Sub

    Private Sub Button1_Click(ByVal sender As System.Object, ByVal e As System.EventArgs) Handles Button1.Click
        ' Check to see if button has been clicked already
        If Button1.Text = "X" Or Button1.Text = "O" Then Return
        ' If XO = 0 then it is Xs turn, if not it is Os turn
        If intXO = 0 Then
            Button1.Text = "X"
            intXO = 1
            lblMessage.Text = "O is up!"
        Else
            Button1.Text = "O"
            intXO = 0
            lblMessage.Text = "X is up!"
        End If
        ' Is there three in a row?
        Dim ThreeinaRow As Boolean = CheckForWinner(Button1.Text, Button2.Text, Button3.Text, Button4.Text, Button5.Text, Button6.Text, Button7.Text, Button8.Text, Button9.Text)
        If ThreeinaRow = True Then
            If intXO = 1 Then
                lblMessage.Text = "X Wins!"
            Else
```

```vb
                lblMessage.Text = "O Wins!"
            End If
            lblMessage.ForeColor = Color.Green
            GameOver()
            Return
        End If
        ' Let's check to see of the game is a draw
        ' If intDrawGame is 9, it means that all 9 squares have been marked
        intDrawGame += 1
        If intDrawGame = 9 Then
            lblMessage.Text = "Game is a draw - Tie!"
            GameOver()
        End If
    End Sub

    Private Sub Button2_Click(ByVal sender As System.Object, ByVal e As System.EventArgs) Handles Button2.Click
        ' Check to see if button has been clicked already
        If Button2.Text = "X" Or Button2.Text = "O" Then Return
        ' If XO = 0 then it is Xs turn, if not it is Os turn
        If intXO = 0 Then
            Button2.Text = "X"
            intXO = 1
            lblMessage.Text = "O is up!"
        Else
            Button2.Text = "O"
            intXO = 0
            lblMessage.Text = "X is up!"
        End If
        ' Is there three in a row?
        Dim ThreeinaRow As Boolean = CheckForWinner(Button1.Text, Button2.Text, Button3.Text, Button4.Text, Button5.Text, Button6.Text, Button7.Text, Button8.Text, Button9.Text)
        If ThreeinaRow = True Then
            If intXO = 1 Then
                lblMessage.Text = "X Wins!"
            Else
                lblMessage.Text = "O Wins!"
            End If
            lblMessage.ForeColor = Color.Green
            GameOver()
            Return
        End If
        ' Let's check to see of the game is a draw
        ' If intDrawGame is 9, it means that all 9 squares have been marked
        intDrawGame += 1
        If intDrawGame = 9 Then
            lblMessage.Text = "Game is a draw - Tie!"
            GameOver()
        End If
    End Sub

    Private Sub Button3_Click(ByVal sender As System.Object, ByVal e As System.EventArgs) Handles Button3.Click
        ' Check to see if button has been clicked already
        If Button3.Text = "X" Or Button3.Text = "O" Then Return
        ' If XO = 0 then it is Xs turn, if not it is Os turn
        If intXO = 0 Then
```

```vb
            Button3.Text = "X"
            intXO = 1
            lblMessage.Text = "O is up!"
        Else
            Button3.Text = "O"
            intXO = 0
            lblMessage.Text = "X is up!"
        End If
        ' Is there three in a row?
        Dim ThreeinaRow As Boolean = CheckForWinner(Button1.Text, Button2.Text, Button3.Text, Button4.Text, Button5.Text, Button6.Text, Button7.Text, Button8.Text, Button9.Text)
        If ThreeinaRow = True Then
            If intXO = 1 Then
                lblMessage.Text = "X Wins!"
            Else
                lblMessage.Text = "O Wins!"
            End If
            lblMessage.ForeColor = Color.Green
            GameOver()
            Return
        End If
        ' Let's check to see of the game is a draw
        ' If intDrawGame is 9, it means that all 9 squares have been marked
        intDrawGame += 1
        If intDrawGame = 9 Then
            lblMessage.Text = "Game is a draw - Tie!"
            GameOver()
        End If
    End Sub

    Private Sub Button4_Click(ByVal sender As System.Object, ByVal e As System.EventArgs) Handles Button4.Click
        ' Check to see if button has been clicked already
        If Button4.Text = "X" Or Button4.Text = "O" Then Return
        ' If XO = 0 then it is Xs turn, if not it is Os turn
        If intXO = 0 Then
            Button4.Text = "X"
            intXO = 1
            lblMessage.Text = "O is up!"
        Else
            Button4.Text = "O"
            intXO = 0
            lblMessage.Text = "X is up!"
        End If
        ' Is there three in a row?
        Dim ThreeinaRow As Boolean = CheckForWinner(Button1.Text, Button2.Text, Button3.Text, Button4.Text, Button5.Text, Button6.Text, Button7.Text, Button8.Text, Button9.Text)
        If ThreeinaRow = True Then
            If intXO = 1 Then
                lblMessage.Text = "X Wins!"
            Else
                lblMessage.Text = "O Wins!"
            End If
            lblMessage.ForeColor = Color.Green
            GameOver()
            Return
```

```vbnet
        End If
        ' Let's check to see of the game is a draw
        ' If intDrawGame is 9, it means that all 9 squares have been marked
        intDrawGame += 1
        If intDrawGame = 9 Then
            lblMessage.Text = "Game is a draw - Tie!"
            GameOver()
        End If
    End Sub

    Private Sub Button5_Click(ByVal sender As System.Object, ByVal e As System.EventArgs) Handles Button5.Click
        ' Check to see if button has been clicked already
        If Button5.Text = "X" Or Button5.Text = "O" Then Return
        ' If XO = 0 then it is Xs turn, if not it is Os turn
        If intXO = 0 Then
            Button5.Text = "X"
            intXO = 1
            lblMessage.Text = "O is up!"
        Else
            Button5.Text = "O"
            intXO = 0
            lblMessage.Text = "X is up!"
        End If
        ' Is there three in a row?
        Dim ThreeinaRow As Boolean = CheckForWinner(Button1.Text, Button2.Text, Button3.Text, Button4.Text, Button5.Text, Button6.Text, Button7.Text, Button8.Text, Button9.Text)
        If ThreeinaRow = True Then
            If intXO = 1 Then
                lblMessage.Text = "X Wins!"
            Else
                lblMessage.Text = "O Wins!"
            End If
            lblMessage.ForeColor = Color.Green
            GameOver()
            Return
        End If
        ' Let's check to see of the game is a draw
        ' If intDrawGame is 9, it means that all 9 squares have been marked
        intDrawGame += 1
        If intDrawGame = 9 Then
            lblMessage.Text = "Game is a draw - Tie!"
            GameOver()
        End If
    End Sub

    Private Sub Button6_Click(ByVal sender As System.Object, ByVal e As System.EventArgs) Handles Button6.Click
        ' Check to see if button has been clicked already
        If Button6.Text = "X" Or Button6.Text = "O" Then Return
        ' If XO = 0 then it is Xs turn, if not it is Os turn
        If intXO = 0 Then
            Button6.Text = "X"
            intXO = 1
            lblMessage.Text = "O is up!"
        Else
            Button6.Text = "O"
```

```vb
            intXO = 0
            lblMessage.Text = "X is up!"
        End If
        ' Is there three in a row?
        Dim ThreeinaRow As Boolean = CheckForWinner(Button1.Text, Button2.Text, Button3.Text, Button4.Text, Button5.Text, Button6.Text, Button7.Text, Button8.Text, Button9.Text)
        If ThreeinaRow = True Then
            If intXO = 1 Then
                lblMessage.Text = "X Wins!"
            Else
                lblMessage.Text = "O Wins!"
            End If
            lblMessage.ForeColor = Color.Green
            GameOver()
            Return
        End If
        ' Let's check to see of the game is a draw
        ' If intDrawGame is 9, it means that all 9 squares have been marked
        intDrawGame += 1
        If intDrawGame = 9 Then
            lblMessage.Text = "Game is a draw - Tie!"
            GameOver()
        End If
    End Sub

    Private Sub Button7_Click(ByVal sender As System.Object, ByVal e As System.EventArgs) Handles Button7.Click
        ' Check to see if button has been clicked already
        If Button7.Text = "X" Or Button7.Text = "O" Then Return
        ' If XO = 0 then it is Xs turn, if not it is Os turn
        If intXO = 0 Then
            Button7.Text = "X"
            intXO = 1
            lblMessage.Text = "O is up!"
        Else
            Button7.Text = "O"
            intXO = 0
            lblMessage.Text = "X is up!"
        End If
        ' Is there three in a row?
        Dim ThreeinaRow As Boolean = CheckForWinner(Button1.Text, Button2.Text, Button3.Text, Button4.Text, Button5.Text, Button6.Text, Button7.Text, Button8.Text, Button9.Text)
        If ThreeinaRow = True Then
            If intXO = 1 Then
                lblMessage.Text = "X Wins!"
            Else
                lblMessage.Text = "O Wins!"
            End If
            lblMessage.ForeColor = Color.Green
            GameOver()
            Return
        End If
        ' Let's check to see of the game is a draw
        ' If intDrawGame is 9, it means that all 9 squares have been marked
        intDrawGame += 1
        If intDrawGame = 9 Then
```

```vbnet
            lblMessage.Text = "Game is a draw - Tie!"
            GameOver()
        End If
    End Sub

    Private Sub Button8_Click(ByVal sender As System.Object, ByVal e As System.EventArgs) Handles Button8.Click
        ' Check to see if button has been clicked already
        If Button8.Text = "X" Or Button8.Text = "O" Then Return
        ' If XO = 0 then it is Xs turn, if not it is Os turn
        If intXO = 0 Then
            Button8.Text = "X"
            intXO = 1
            lblMessage.Text = "O is up!"
        Else
            Button8.Text = "O"
            intXO = 0
            lblMessage.Text = "X is up!"
        End If
        ' Is there three in a row?
        Dim ThreeinaRow As Boolean = CheckForWinner(Button1.Text, Button2.Text, Button3.Text, Button4.Text, Button5.Text, Button6.Text, Button7.Text, Button8.Text, Button9.Text)
        If ThreeinaRow = True Then
            If intXO = 1 Then
                lblMessage.Text = "X Wins!"
            Else
                lblMessage.Text = "O Wins!"
            End If
            lblMessage.ForeColor = Color.Green
            GameOver()
            Return
        End If
        ' Let's check to see of the game is a draw
        ' If intDrawGame is 9, it means that all 9 squares have been marked
        intDrawGame += 1
        If intDrawGame = 9 Then
            lblMessage.Text = "Game is a draw - Tie!"
            GameOver()
        End If
    End Sub

    Private Sub Button9_Click(ByVal sender As System.Object, ByVal e As System.EventArgs) Handles Button9.Click
        ' Check to see if button has been clicked already
        If Button9.Text = "X" Or Button9.Text = "O" Then Return
        ' If XO = 0 then it is Xs turn, if not it is Os turn
        If intXO = 0 Then
            Button9.Text = "X"
            intXO = 1
            lblMessage.Text = "O is up!"
        Else
            Button9.Text = "O"
            intXO = 0
            lblMessage.Text = "X is up!"
        End If
        ' Is there three in a row?
```

```vb
        Dim ThreeinaRow As Boolean = CheckForWinner(Button1.Text, Button2.Text, Button3.Text, Button4.Text, Button5.Text, Button6.Text, Button7.Text, Button8.Text, Button9.Text)
        If ThreeinaRow = True Then
            If intXO = 1 Then
                lblMessage.Text = "X Wins!"
            Else
                lblMessage.Text = "O Wins!"
            End If
            lblMessage.ForeColor = Color.Green
            GameOver()
            Return
        End If
        ' Let's check to see of the game is a draw
        ' If intDrawGame is 9, it means that all 9 squares have been marked
        intDrawGame += 1
        If intDrawGame = 9 Then
            lblMessage.Text = "Game is a draw - Tie!"
            GameOver()
        End If
    End Sub

    Private Sub btnClear_Click(ByVal sender As System.Object, ByVal e As System.EventArgs) Handles btnClear.Click
        ' Clear and enable the buttons
        Button1.Enabled = True
        Button2.Enabled = True
        Button3.Enabled = True
        Button4.Enabled = True
        Button5.Enabled = True
        Button6.Enabled = True
        Button7.Enabled = True
        Button8.Enabled = True
        Button9.Enabled = True
        Button1.Text = ""
        Button2.Text = ""
        Button3.Text = ""
        Button4.Text = ""
        Button5.Text = ""
        Button6.Text = ""
        Button7.Text = ""
        Button8.Text = ""
        Button9.Text = ""
        ' Reset our global Class variables to Zero
        intXO = 0
        intDrawGame = 0
        ' Let X know they are first to play
        lblMessage.Text = "X is up"
        lblMessage.ForeColor = Color.Black
    End Sub
End Class
```

Let's play!

Remember to Save! = ![save icons]

Step 4: Test and Tune It

Testing and tuning your program is running it to see if everything is working the way you think it should and more importantly if your program is working the way you defined it in Step 2.

Now let's Test! Start your program,

Press F5   or   [Debug ▸ Start Debugging (F5)]   or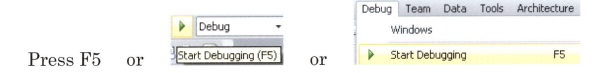

Your program appears:

X is up. Click a square (button) and X will be placed in the button you clicked.

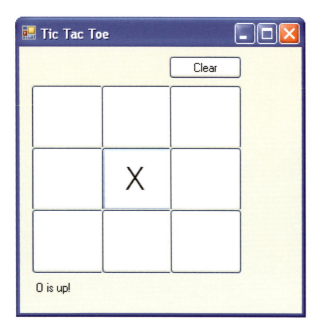

Now O is up so click a button where you want an O to appear.

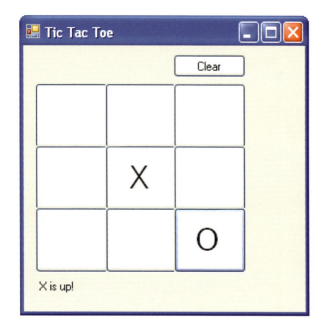

Continue on –

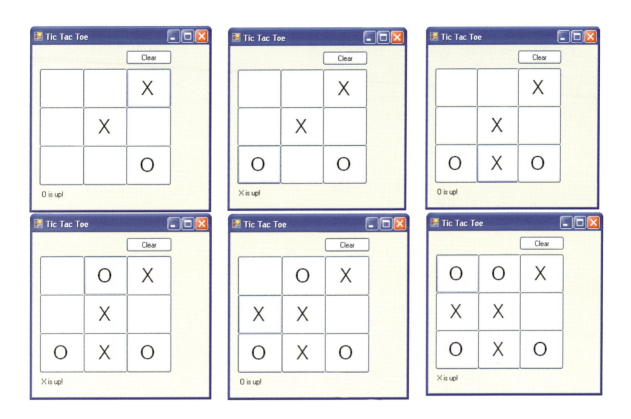

And if you put an X in the last square …

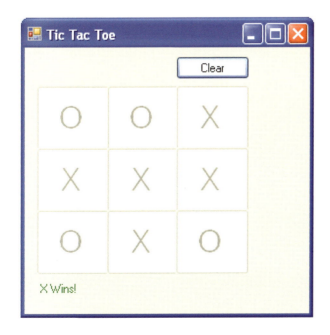

X Wins! So far, our program behaves just as we expected it to.

Click Clear

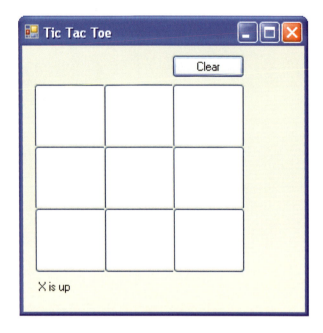

Clear makes all the buttons enabled and blank, and shows X is up. Click Clear to start a new game.

Let's repeat the same sequence as before but instead of X winning, lets create a draw.

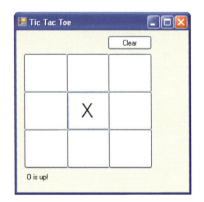 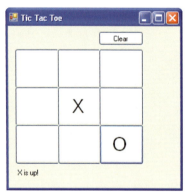 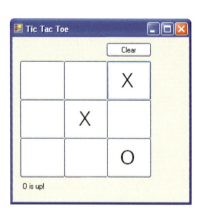

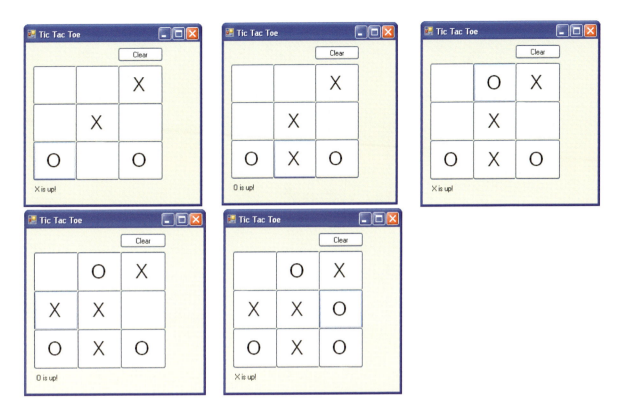

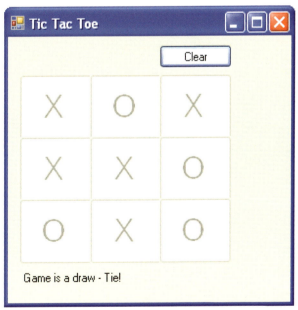

The game is a Tie, there are no three in a row, and the program tells us exactly just what we want.

Test three Os in a row – 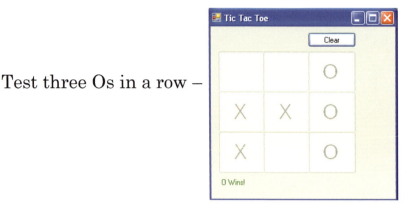 It works!

To test the program thoroughly, you would want to test each type of three in a row, for Xs and for Os.

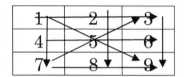

If you tried all the combinations and each worked as you expected, then you know your program is well tested and ready to give to others to play.

So what is Tuning? Tuning is when you see something you don't like and modify it to what you feel is better. This can be in the way the program looks or the way it works. For example, we might want to make the Fonts bigger in the buttons, or if they are X, make them Blue and if O, make them red. In the code, we can see a lot of repetitive items in the code for each button – maybe we can split more of this code into Methods that we can call so that our button code is much smaller. Tuning is just making your program work better.

Step 5: Document It

Documenting can mean several things, including:

- Documenting your code by adding comments
- Creating a Help file for the user that explains how the program works
- Writing a manual for the user to read that explains how the program works

We have done a good job of documenting our code with comments but it is always good to add a paragraph at the top of the program that tells any programmer looking at the code who wrote it, when it was written, any changes you have made over time and why you wrote the program. If we were to add a paragraph at the top, it might look like:

```
' **********************************************************************
' Tic Tac Toe
' This program lets two players play the game of Tic Tac Toe which allows
' each user to place an X or O on any unused square and whoever gets three
' in a row first, wins.
' Written by Timothy Busbice
' Originally written on 4/27/10
' **********************************************************************
Public Class Form1
    Public intXO As Integer
    Public intDrawGame As Integer

Private Sub Form1_Load(ByVal sender As System.Object, ByVal e As System.EventArgs)
```

Code documentation does not always have to be very detailed, just enough to give someone else basic information about who and why the program was written, and what the code does.

User help can come in different forms from very detailed Help files that takes its own programming to simple information within the program. For our help information, let's create a second form that tells the user how to use the program. To start, go to the Visual Studio and click the menu Project > Add Windows Form:

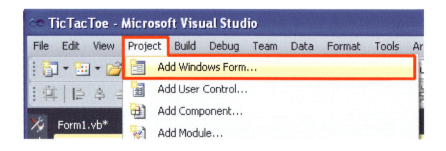

The Add Windows Form screen will pop up:

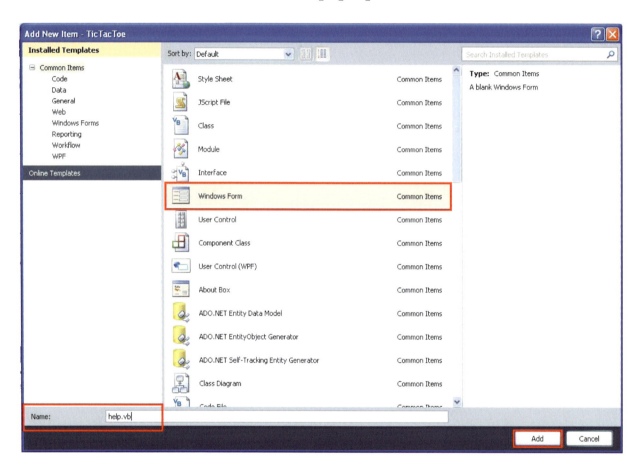

Change the name to *help.vb* and click Add.

You will now see your new form help.vb and you will notice over to the very right, the help.vb in the Explorer.

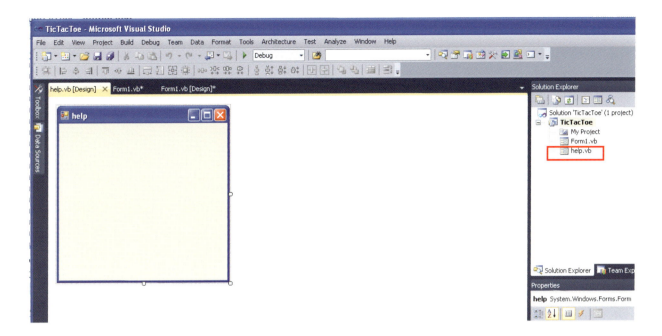

I change my form help.vb Text to Player Help.

On our help.vb form all we want to do is to tell the user how to play the game and after they are finished, allow them to exit. To add the instructions, place a label on the form, name it lblhelp and remove the Text. Once you click off the label, it will seem to disappear but it is there.

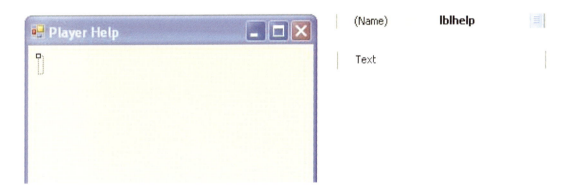

Double-click the form and create the form_load method:

```
Private Sub help_Load(ByVal sender As System.Object, ByVal e As System.EventArgs) Handles MyBase.Load

End Sub
```

In the help_Load Method, put your information on how to play into your label lblhelp. I did the following:

```
Private Sub help_Load(ByVal sender As System.Object, ByVal e As System.EventArgs) Handles MyBase.Load
    lblhelp.Text = "Tic Tac Toe" + Environment.NewLine + Environment.NewLine
    lblhelp.Text += "To play this game, it takes two players." + Environment.NewLine
    lblhelp.Text += "Each player must decide to be either X or O." + Environment.NewLine
    lblhelp.Text += "X goes first by clicking on any square. Then" + Environment.NewLine
    lblhelp.Text += "O clicks on any square that does not have X on" + Environment.NewLine
    lblhelp.Text += "it. Then X clicks on an open square, then O." + Environment.NewLine
    lblhelp.Text += "This continues until either player X or O gets" + Environment.NewLine
    lblhelp.Text += "three in a row or all the squares are used." + Environment.NewLine
    lblhelp.Text += "If no one gets three in a row, the game is " + Environment.NewLine
    lblhelp.Text += "declared a tie." + Environment.NewLine
End Sub
```

In the code above, you can see that you can concatenate or join strings by using += so the first assigned string to lblhelp.Text is = but every string assignment after that is += which adds the strings to the same label and allows the label to grow. Also, at the end of each string, we put `Environment.NewLine` which puts in a linefeed. If we did not put in a linefeed, we would get a string that runs off the form and you could not see what it says.

Last on this form, let's add an Close button to end the form after we have read the help. We will name it btnClose and change the Text to Close.

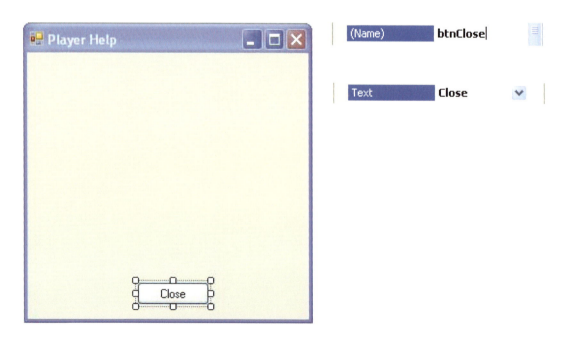

Double-Click btnClose. Enter the following code: `Me.Hide();`

```vb
Private Sub btnClose_Click(ByVal sender As System.Object, ByVal e As System.EventArgs) Handles btnClose.Click
    Me.Hide()
End Sub
```

Now your Help form is complete but we need to access it. Go back to your Form1 form and add a Help button. You can access Form1.vb by clicking on it at the tab on the top or selecting it from the Solution Explorer on the right side of your workbench.

Add the button at the bottom and name it btnHelp. Change the Text to Help.

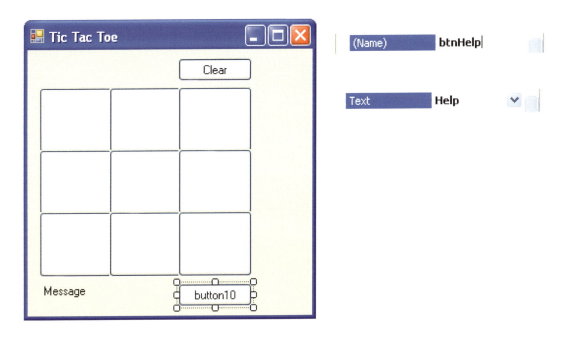

Double-click the btnHelp button and add the code to show the help.vb form.

```
    Private Sub btnHelp_Click(ByVal sender As System.Object, ByVal e As System.EventArgs) Handles btnHelp.Click
        Dim FormHelp As help = New help()
        FormHelp.Show()
    End Sub
```

To show the help.vb form, we need to instantiate the form and then show it. The `Dim FormHelp As help = New help()` code instantiates the form and `FormHelp.Show()` shows the form.

Let's run:

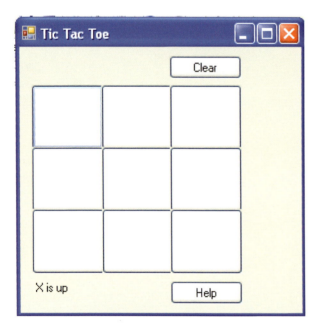

Click Help and should see something like:

Click Close and the help.vb form will go away.
This is a simple way to document how your program is supposed to be used. You have also just learned how to open and close other forms in your program.

Remember to Save! =

Step 6: Implement It

Implementing means to set up your program for others to use. To create an executable program, we use the menu. You will notice a little drop down list that is part of the menu that should show Debug:

Click the drop down and choose Release:

Then click on the menu item Build > Build Tic Tac Toe

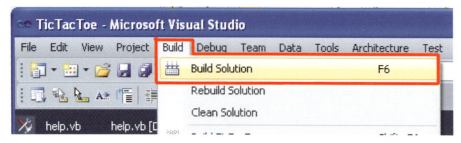

If all went well, you should see that the Build Succeeded at the very bottom of the screen.

Now you have an executable program you can give to anyone to run. You can find your program on your hard drive under where you stored the program. It would look something like:

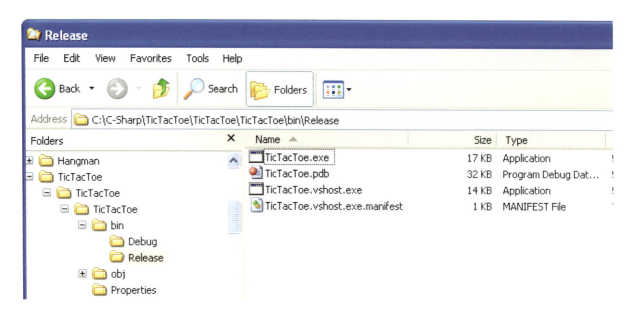

In our case, TicTacToe.exe is all you need. You can copy this and give to your friends. If you double-click it, the program will run.

Notice that in the folders, there is a folder called Debug and Release. If you change your Visual Studio workbench back to Debug in the little drop down list, you can modify your program and not effect the program you want to give to your friends until it is ready to give to them. Visual Studio allows you to have two versions: Debug or your test version, Release or your production version.

Last, I would like to add that there is usually a seventh (it) step in our Waterfall Model and that is "Maintain it". Program maintenance is usually done when you have a program that many people use and the program requires changes from time to time. The Maintain step is essentially Steps 1 through 6 over and over again for any new program changes.

More Fun!

Here are some suggestions to enhance your program. Try these and figure out how to program:

- How would you create a program where you would play against the computer? Think on how to do this by using the random function to look at a button, check if an X or O exists in that button (square) and if so, do another random generation until you find an empty square.

Chapter 4 Definition Review

Waterfall model
The **waterfall model** is a way to organize your program development to make sure you follow steps to build successful programs. There are Six steps:

        Step 1: Learn *It*
        Step 2: Design *It*
        Step 3: Code *It*
        Step 4: Test and Tune *It*
        Step 5: Document *It*
        Step 6: Implement *It*

Function
A **Function** is a Method that is declared as a data type and returns a value. Visual Basic comes with many built-in functions that a programmer can use that are comprised of all types of common utilities.

Executable
An **Executable** program is a complied version of your code that you can give to others and they can play on their computers.

5. The Beginning

You have learned a great deal of information by going through this book and programming the examples. Best of all, you now know how computers are programmed. Even though the examples you have completed are simple, all programs are simple at their smallest components. A big program is made up of many small programs that are added together. We can see a little of this in our Tic Tac Toe program when we setup our Methods that were called by other Methods.

Visual Basic is one of the most prevalent computer languages used in the world. Anyone that learns Visual Basic becomes part of a worldwide club of highly skilled developers. You are now well on your way as a member of this exclusive club. Congratulations!

You can make a computer do just about anything with Visual Basic. I encourage you to explore the many controls in the toolbox and learn all the namespaces you can add on to your programs. You can draw, show pictures, you can talk to other devices, you can play music, and you can make a robot wander, all within a Visual Basic program. So program and play and you will be able to create some awesome applications.

Download the code used in this book and get other good information at http://www.compscikids.com.

But always have fun!

Index

Array, 79
Bold, 15
Button, 8
`CInt`, 40
Classes, 28
Client, 22, 25
Code *It*, 80, 134
Color palette, 16
Comments, 29, 44
Controls, 8, 24
Curly Brackets, 64
Data Types, 45
Debug, 44
debugging, 35
Design, 80
Design *It*, 80, 134
Document *It*, 80, 134
EasyGame, 6, 9, 25, 35, 67
ELSE, 40
Enable Property, 79
Enabled = false, 61
Enabled property, 61
Executable, 131
F5, 20
Font, 14
ForeColor, 16
Form, 8, 24
Function, 36, 44, 98
Hangman, iv, 46, 47, 48, 63, 68, 72, 78
IF ... THEN ... ELSE, 30, 39, 44
Implement *It*, 80, 134
in class, 64
In Class Variable, 79
instantiation, 37
InStr, 67, 79
integer, 37
Intellisense, 31
IsNumeric, 36
Labels, 8
Language, 3, 23
Learn *It*, 80, 134
Learning, 80
MaxLength, 18
Methods, 28
Microsoft, ii, 2, 4, 20, 23, 26, 30, 45
Namespace, 28
Namespace, Classes and Methods, 44
NewProject, 5
Ordinal, 63
Presentation, 25
Presentation Layer, 22
Program, 3, 23
Properties, 10, 11, 12, 24
Property Manager, 10
Random, 37
Random function, 37
Red X, 21, 33
Select, 79
Select Case, 69
Size, 15
Statement(s), 3, 23
Template, 5, 24, 47, 85
Test and Tune *It*, 80, 134
Text Boxes, 8
Tic Tac Toe, iv, 80, 81, 86, 125, 128, 132, 135
Toggling between your Form and your Code, 26
tools, 4
Variables, 44
Visible property, 61
Visual Basic, ii, 1, 3, 4, 5, 6, 8, 23, 38, 38, 43, 44, 45, 47, 63, 70, 75, 85, 98, 134, 135
Visual Studio, ii, 2, 4, 6, 23, 25, 46, 84, 125, 133
Waterfall model, 80
Windows Forms Application, 5, 47, 85
workshop, 4

CPSIA information can be obtained at www.ICGtesting.com
Printed in the USA
LVIW01n2322310715
448475LV00006B/65